Fragments of Else Where

Book 2: Faith, Hope & Prayer

Henry Anastasi

Dedication

Nothing worthwhile in life comes without effort, and my strength has always drawn from those who cared.
With deep appreciation, I extend my gratitude to everyone whose presence and encouragement made this collection possible.

To My Mother
My heartfelt thanks to my mother, whose steady guidance lit my path. She has been my anchor and my inspiration—my light in every shadowed hour.

To Janet B.M.
To my dear friend Janet, who listened with patience and without judgment, no matter the hour.
Your faith in my words rekindled my passion whenever it flickered. You reminded me to write—and to keep writing.

To Creative Influences
To the many voices, seen and unseen, whose ideas and spirit helped shape these poems.
Your influence has been both quiet and profound—woven through every line.

To the Many
To the countless people whose kindness, presence, and impact I could never have done without.
You are felt in every page.

To God
Above all, to God—my source of purpose, peace, and being. Without Him, none of this would exist.

Table of Contents

Dedication ii
Table of Contents iii
WHEN MIRACLES COME TRUE 2
VIOLATED TRUST 6
FAITHFUL TO THE END 10
THE TRUTH 14
FACE THE TRUTH 18
SCATTERED TO THE WIND 21
DEEDS, NOT WORDS 25
TOMORROW WILL BE OK 30
GIVE US THIS DAY 33
IL-BANDIERA TA-MALTA (The Maltese Flag) 36
THE FIRE OF DESTRUCTION 39
SHADOWS IN THE FLAME 43
HOPE I DIDN'T WAKE YOU 46
THE DEMONS WITHIN 49
WALK AWAY 53
THE NEW ME 56
THE DREAMS I PROMISED YOU 60
AS I STOP TO COUNT MY BLESSINGS 64
IN THE DEPTH OF NOTHINGNESS 67
ASTRAL PLAINS 71
THE CLAIRVOYANT 77
PSYCHIC REALM 81
A DREAM OF THEIR OWN 86
FLYING 30,000 FEET 90
YOU ARE MY SUNSHINE 95

LETTING GO	100
GOOD MORNING BEAUTIFUL	106
DISTANCE	110
THE BOND	114
SOME NIGHTS	117
RAGE AND FURY	121
WHILE THE WORLD SLEEPS	127
YOU ARE THE REASON	131
MIRACLES DO COME TRUE	134
UNSPOKEN	138
THE UNSEEN THREAD	142
GRANDMAS KITCHEN	147
IS-SALEB TA MALTIN (Maltese Cross)	151
BETRAYAL	154
TULIPS	157
MAMA TOLD ME	161
SOMETHING INSIDE	164
FOLLOW YOUR DREAM	168
WHEN DESTINY CALLS	172
WHAT SHE WANTED, WASN'T WORDS	175
PAY IT FORWARD	180
SOMETIMES ITS HARD	184
LOOK INSIDE	187
X'HEMM MOHBI - (What Is Hidden)	192
WALKING ON EGGSHELLS	195
LET ME DOWN SOFTLY	201
GIVE ME A SECOND CHANCE	206
SEASONS OF MY LIFE	210

MY DUSTBIN DREAMS	213
THE FURY OF THE SEA	219
WALK IN MY SHOES	223
WHO I AM	229
THE POET	232
THIS IS ME	235
TO THE EDGE Of ETERNITY	238
THE MIRROR	241
TEN THOUSAND REASONS	246
THE LAST CHAPTER	250
TODAY I'M PUSHING BACK	254
STANDING ROOM ONLY	262
MY UNIVERSE	268
UNWRITTEN	272
RECURRING DREAMS	275
A BOTTLE AND ME	279
NEVER ENOUGH	284
MY REDEEMER KING	287
A WORLD	290
AFTER THE FIRE	293
THE DAY THE COLOURS FADED	297
PARENTHOOD	302
BEAUTIFUL IN WHITE	308
SOMETHING ABOUT YOU	311
TIME TRAVEL	314
AS I LAY AND PONDER	317
BEFORE YOU GO	321
SOMETIMES I WANNA QUIT	325

MONEY CAN'T BUY…	329
NATURES GIFT	333
MY SON	337
NEVER SAY NEVER	341
A BIRTHDAY WISH	346
WHAT THE DEAF MAN HEARD	350
IF ONLY	353
DON'T GIVE UP	361
A WOMAN'S SCENT	364
YOU'LL NEVER KNOW	369
STOLEN LOVE	374
STOLEN SILENCE	378
NEVER GIVE UP ON US	382
WAKE ME FROM THIS SLEEP	386
CHASING THE DREAMS	389
I DON'T KNOW	393
HIDING BEHIND THE PAST	398
THIS BATTLE I MUST FIGHT	402
RENO AND I	408
HAUNTED MANSION	414
LOVE UNREQUITED	420
A PROMISE	426
YOU'VE ALWAYS BEEN	429
NOTHING ELSE MATTERED	433
BACK IN TIME	437
THE ASHES	440
THE HARDEST THING	445
STUFF IT	449

OPEN BOOK	455
ONE MORE CHANCE	460
ANNOYING SISTERS	464
WISH ME LUCK	469
LEAVE, WHAT WAS YESTERDAY	473
PHYSICAL ATTRACTION	476
CAN WE START OVER AGAIN	480
THIS POEM	484
NATURE'S TREASURES	487
WATER	491
MIRROR	495
I SPY	499
WE ALL BLEED THE SAME	503
MY NIGHTMARE VISITORS	507
YOUR SONG	511
HANDLE WITH CARE	514
REFLECTIONS ON THE WINDOW	517
ACCEPT ME FOR WHAT I AM	520
DARKNESS IN THE WOODS	523
RUBBER BAND	526
DREAM AFTER DREAM	530
THE FARMER AND THE SEED	533
SOMEONE DIFFERENT	536
THROUGH THE WINDOW	541
KOALA UP IN THE TREES	545
YOU'RE NEVER TOO FAR	549
HAND IN HAND	553
TIME FREEZE	556

WHAT MAY LIE AHEAD 560
SOMEWHERE ONLY WE KNOW 565
THAT FIRST KISS 570
SOMETIMES 574
BROKEN DREAMS 577
BURNING WORDS 581
HIS FINAL POEM 585
THE PAINTING 589
THIS SMALL TOWN 593
FOOTPRINTS IN THE SAND 597
WHAT ONCE WAS 601
WHAT REALLY MATTERS 605
BOWING TO THE QUIET LIGHT 609

WHEN MIRACLES COME TRUE

We Walk This Earth In Wonderment
Of All That Is Around Us
But Never Have We Stopped To Wonder
Or In God, Did We Ever Trust

When Miracles Come True, In
The Light Of A New Morn
When Half The World Is Sleeping
The Other, Awaits A Child To Be Born

The Miracles Of Life
At The Sounds Of A Baby's First Cry
Eyes Half Open, A Smile Upon Its First Sight
A Kiss On Her Forehead, That Cannot Be Denied

Her First Glimpse, The Miracles Around Her
She Doesn't Yet Quite Know
Of What Life Has In Store
Or What Hurdles, Life Will Throw

When Miracles Come True
I Marvel At Life's Creation
From A Seed We Grow, And Like A Giant Oak,
Makes Way, The Next Generation

The Beauty That Surrounds Us
Much We've Taken For Granted
But None So Much
As Every Tree, That Was Ever Planted

Faith, What Drives Us To Believe That
Something So Ordinary, Can Be A Miracle
A New Day, Turning Into The Night
Or Perhaps Something Unseen, Invisible

When Miracles Come True
A Celebration, A Feast To Which We Toast
At Times, Cannot Be Explained
And Times, We'll Forget, What Really Matters Most

The How's And Whys, And The Reasons
Does Anyone Really Care
Like How We Came To Be
In A Vast Universe Or How We Got Here

With My Eyes Wide Open, I'm Left In Awe
At This Worldly Sphere
To Which Only A Miracle Can Explain
And To Mankind Right Now, Seems Unclear

When Miracles Come True,
To Breathe, Solely, Is A Miracle Alone
And So Too Is Dying, A Miracle Of Life
As We Make Way To A Journey Unknown

Miracles Around Us Every Day,
From The, What We Cannot Perceive
To The Ones Underneath Our Noses
Those At Times, So Hard To Believe

When Miracles Come True
An Act Of Something Much Greater
We'll Pray To The Skies And Heaven
And Thank, The All Mighty Creator

VIOLATED TRUST

I Once Believed In Honesty Until I Met You
You Had Me Believing You Were Special
But In The End, Just Violated Trust
A Cheating Lying Vessel

Filled With Promises That Were Broken
Gifts You Bought From A Dollar Store
Hiding Behind The Truth, Blemished
Left Me Thinking There Was More

I Hung Around, Thinking Maybe You'd Change
But Deception, Written All Over Your Face
You Told Me I Was Your Everything
But Just Like Lucifer, Falling Out Of Grace

Could You Not See The Anguish
That I Was Stranded With
When You Took My Hand
Was Starting To Believe Your Love Was A Myth

You Violated My Belief
You Violated My Trust
The Hurt, Much More Than I Could Bear
Anything You Gave, Just Turned To Dust

You Told Me I Was The Pearl Of Your Oyster
Now Live With Battered Bruises
I Longed To Have You Back
Without The Tarnished Promises

To Have And To Hold, Words I Treasured
I Got More Than I Bargained For
And In Sickness And In Health
In The End, It Was My Heart Your Tore

I Long To See, Two Hearts Etched Upon The Sand
And There To Stay, Till It's Washed Away
But My Dreams Are Just That
Reality, Is Never Really That Way

You Are Leaving The Best Part Of Us
Where Two Becomes One
We Once Had That, I Then Realised
But, As Of Now… Nothing… None

Our Journey Will Soon Be Over
But What Will Remain, Only Violated Trust
I Know It Wont Be Easy
And Time's All I Have To Adjust

You Once Said You Loved Me
And I Really Did Truly Believe
But, How Can I Now
I Was Then, Just A Child, Still Very Naive

The Hurt Of The Past, Can Never Be Washed Away
You've Nailed Me To The Cross
With Your Violated Trust
You Walk Away Now, Honey…Will Truly Be Your Loss

FAITHFUL TO THE END

I Will Fight For Your Honour, Forever And Always
If You're Wondering If I'll Be True
Yes Faithful To The End
So Much More Than You Ever Knew

I Will Lay My Life Before You
Walk On Hot Embers, If That Means You Will Be Mine
I Will Promise My Faith Till The End
My Love For You, One Cannot Define

My Life Is Nothing Without You
I Will Surrender It Before A Firing Squad
And Plead My Sincerity
When I Am Standing Before God

There Is Nothing That I Will Hide
If It Means That I Belong To You
Because I Will Be Faithful Till The End
Though It Meant Torture, They Put Me Through

I Will Be Your Sacrificial Lamb
Slain Upon A Sacred Shrine
And Let My Blood Fill The Cups
As My True Love Sign

I Will Not Scream In Pain
But Fight For What Is Right
I Will Be Faithful Till The End
In Due Time That We Both Follow The Light

If We Should Part And Lose Direction
No Time Or Space Can Keep Us Away
For I Long To Embrace In Your Arms
And With You I'll Endeavor To Stay

You Tested My Trust, Yet I Came Through
Told You, I'd Be Faithful Till The End
You Questioned Me About Loyalty
But The Truth, I Would Never Bend

Forever And Always
That Time Is Of No Essence
When I'm With You
Time Stands Still, Now In The Presence

There Is So Much To Share
We Have Nothing To Conceal
Our Love's Like And Open Book
Like A Fairytale Story, So Surreal

Are We living A Fantasy Dream
Everything Seems Just Perfect
I Don't Want To Wake Up
And Never To Know, What To Expect

All That I Can Offer
My Faithfulness Till The End
Walk Through Life, Through Thick And Thin
To Be Your One And Only, This I Intend

For This Time We Have, Is Precious
Moments, So Dearly Cherished
Will Enjoy Till The End
Before That Day Comes, That We will Perish

THE TRUTH

We Cannot Hide From The Truth
But Some Choose To Masquerade It
And Smear It With Lies
But To This, Will They Ever Admit

By Nature I'm An Optimist
The Truth Will Always Prevail
Whatever, However It Is Said
Take Caution, Your Treachery, I Will Unveil

I Am Not Naïve, Of What Goes Around
What You Say, May Never Be Trusted
And Only Decorate, Just So To Conceal
But In The End, It's Just Lies You've Constructed

I Refuse To Be The Victim Of Lies
Through Words So Cautiously Scripted
Your Words, I Cannot Trust
And The Truth, Like A Flower, Wilted

Your Actions, Do Not Justify The Truth
These, That Would Never Lie
When You Came To Me
Why Would You, No Reason To Wonder Why

To Laugh Behind My Back
Perhaps Thinking, I Would Never Notice
What Came To Really Matter
Was The Camouflage Upon Your Surface

They Say Time, Will Unveil The Truth
From The Gossip, The Lies,
But The Cloak You Came To Wear
Could Not Shield You From This Disguise

You Pretend On Being Someone You're Not
But All You Are, Just The Jaded Truth
I Knew You Once, Long Ago
But You've Not Changed, Since Our Youth

Take A Look Around You
What Do You See,
You Cannot Say, For You're Too Blinded
To Ever Be Set Free

The Truth Lay Bleeding, Beneath
Every Word That You Would Say
In The End, It Will Perish
Slowly To Wither, To Decay

When I Saw You Yesterday,
Hiding Behind Your Fake Smile
Your Lies, Penetrated Like An Arrow
I Knew From Here, We Could Not Reconcile

Like A Dagger Deep Inside Me
You Scored
My Heart In Tatters, Shreded
Was It My Feelings You Tried To Ignore

My Love, My Illusions You Destroyed,
An Attempt To Run From The Truth
But Try As You Did
Could Never Rightly Soothe

Please Leave, Never To Return,
There's Nothing More To Cherish
No Memories Of The Cuddles We Shared
In The End, The Truth, Was Sure To Perish

FACE THE TRUTH

In The Days I Wandered
Far From You, Your Voice
Did Echo My Fortress
Mind
My Loneliness Crept In, But
For A Moment Of Time, You Briefly
Appeared
A Panic I Could Not Contain
I Dreaded, You Leaving Me
Behind
Never Ever Seeing You Again
Was Something Much I
Feared
I Knew, In That Moment
A Time To Face The
Truth
You Weren't Coming Back
This, Had To
Accept
Gone Are The Days, Of Frolic
In The Times Of Our
Youth
There, Together We Cuddled And
Kissed, When As One We
Slept

I Searched For You Through
The Far, Endless, Distant
Plain
To Wash Away My Tears, And
A Broken Heart That Needed
Mending
Only Now, Scattered Images Of You
These, Which Barely
Remain
To Face The Truth, And
Accept That What Is, Just Memories
Never-Ending
The Days That Were, Those Yester-Years
When You Took My Pains
You Shielded With A
Kiss
But You Are Now So Far
Out Of Touch, Little More To
Achieve
To Take My Hand, To Replenish
A Lost Love, And Continue Like
This
I'm Left To Face The Truth, And
Hope One Day, Soon, In You, I Will
Believe

SCATTERED TO THE WIND

When My Body Has Breathed Its
Last, And I Am Laid To Rest In
Peace
Do Not Mourn My Departure
I Am Merely Eternally
Asleep
I Know You Will Be With Me
I Know We'll Be Together Some
Day
For When My Spirit, From This
Body Comes To Be
Released
Then God, My Soul, In His
Kingdom Will
Keep
Let My Ashes Be Placed
Within A Gilted Urn, Next
To Where My Picture
Lays
Then I'll Ask To Be Scattered
To The Southern
Wind

Into The Rising Swirls,
Where St Peter Stands,
There, I'll Enter The Pearly
Gates
To Face An Angelic Jury With
God And Jesus, The
Supreme
To Be Judged For Times
I Have Deviated, The Times I Have
Sinned
May Take A Lifetime Or A
Blink Of An Eye, To Determine My
Fate
My Life's Big Picture That Hangs
In Gods Majestic Grand
Scheme
In Life, There Is Dying,
And In Dying, There Is
Life
A New Life Of Change
A New Life To Make
Amends
Let Me Be Scattered To The Winds
High Above The
Skies

This Note I Leave, A Testament

A Will, Please Give To My Darling

Wife

My Deepest Devotion, To

Her, My Love

Extends

When I Am Scattered To The Winds

Let My Spirits From My Body

Rise

DEEDS, NOT WORDS

In Life, Promises Are Often Broken
And Trust, Seldom Met
If Only Deeds Were Honoured
Then Words, Might We Forget

Deeds, Not Words Paint
The Truest Story
Upon A Woven Canvas
With Actions, That Fills Us With Glory

For The Whispers Will Fade
And Actions Shall Stand
When Promises, No Longer Kept
And Deeds, Were Never Planned

So Let Your Actions Be A Guiding Force,
When Words, Can Often Deceive
Let Your Deeds Forever Endure
With Lasting Moments, You Can Believe

Truly Said, "Actions, Speak
Louder Than Words"
Especially Those Without Meaning
And Promises Often Go Unheard

We Sometimes Dream
Of Making Changes
But Deeds, Not Words
Will Succeed, To Various Stages

We May Fail As We May Try
But Good Intentions Never Die
We May Stumble And Fall
Getting Back Up, And So Again We Try

Words Can Give False Hope
And The Promises Of Deeds Never Surface
We Believe Something Great Can Be Achieved
Only If It's There To Be Of Service

I've Often Heard "I'll Do It Later"
But Later Just Never Arrives
It's Been Diffused In Drift Of Time
Then Suddenly Fails To Survive

These Are Words Without Actions
And Such, Are Only Dreams,
Tending To Fade, When Reality Sets In
This Be True, So It Seems

And Dreams Without Deeds
Are Like The Shadows Of The Night
Disappearing As The Day
Is Brought Into Light

Don't Promise What You Cannot Deliver
You Wrote On A Card. "I Love You" When We Met
Then Ran Away With Another
How Quickly Our Love, You Did Forget

Deeds, Not Words
You Found So Hard To Accept
Whilst These You Seemingly Lacked
And Your Honesty, You Rarely Kept

How Can We Live On, What Might Be
But Seldom, On What Is Real
I Don't Want To Live On Expectations
And Nothing In Return For How I Feel

We Live In A World Shaped By Deeds, Not Words
Where Ideas Are Empty
Till Fruition Comes To Surface
These Hands Have Built What You Now See

So Let Our Deeds Withstand Eternity
Making Every Word Count And Intended
For Deeds Without Actions
Like A Hollow Promise Can Never Be Mended

TOMORROW WILL BE OK

Every day, Is That Same Old Story
I Lie In Bed, Not Wanting To Get Up
Could There Be More To This Life I'm Living
No Dreams To Fill My Cup

If I Could Seek Into A Crystal Ball
I Will Know If Tomorrow Will Be Ok
I'd Want To Leave This Day Behind
From It, I Would Run Away

They Tell Me Tomorrow Will Be Ok
But How Can I Believe Them
When Lies Upon Lies, They Throw At Me
And Find, It's From You They Stem

You Lead Me To Believe Of A Brighter Future
The One That Starts With You And I
But A Little Voice In My Head
He'll Only Make You Cry

Tomorrow Will Be Ok, Kept On Believing
Coz Nothing's As Bad, As What It Is Today
A New Day, A New Chapter
A New Beginning, Ill Hope And Pray

I Will Escape My Life Of Old
The One That Ended With You
For Somewhere In Tomorrow
Will Forget, What You Put Me Through

And When Tomorrow Knocks On My Door
I'll Open To Find What's Close Behind
Will Welcome It In
And Hope, Is That I'll Wish To Find

Tomorrow Will Start Fresh, Anew
A Blank Page, With No Concerns, No Fears,
One That's Not Yet Written,
One To Which I Will Not Shed Tears
Yes! Tomorrow Will Be Ok

GIVE US THIS DAY

Give Us This Day, As We Wait Upon Tomorrow
Pave The Paths, Away From Harm
That We May Seek To Repay You
For Keeping Us Safe And Calm

I Ask Not For Myself,
But For Those Who Have Nothing
For Those Of No Shelter
Or Family To Share In The Loving

Give Us This Day, That We May Care,
For Others, With Misfortunes,
To The Loved Ones, They May Have Lost
Seeking Only Comfort, Not Worldly Fortunes

Help Them Find Their Way Through Misery
And Give Them The Guidance
To Get Though Their Darkness
And Hand In Hand we'll Stand Beside Us

Give Us This Day, So Never Will We Thirst
The Bread Of Life, So Never Shall We Hunger
The Strength That We May Believe
The Courage, That We Mayn't Wander

Give Us This Day, That Salvation Be Upon Us
To Be Freed From Any Wrong Doings
When Our Time Has Been Complete
We'll Leave This Body, From Its Wretched Ruins

Give Us This Day To Teach Us Sacrifice
That We Learn To Understand, To Be Human
To Weep In Sadness, To Laugh In Joy
To Love One Another, Man Or Woman

Give Us This Day, That We Never Give Up
On Ourselves, Family And Friends
With Those Whom We Care For
With Those, Upon Who We Depend

In The Roads Of Life, We'll Face Many Hurdles
This, The Journey We Must Make
Where They May Lead, Who Can Say
But Along The Way, It's The Risks We Must Take

IL-BANDIERA TA-MALTA
(The Maltese Flag)

Flying High On A Mast
Into The Mediterranean Breeze
That Blows From The East
Overlooks The Grand Harbour's Blue Seas

Red And White, The George Cross Upper Left
The Flag Of The Maltese Isle
Embraces Its Rich Culture
And People Sharing A Smile

Il-Bandiera Ta Malta, Just A Linen Cloth
That Sways In The Fragrant Air
To A Reminder How We Fought For Glory
And The Proudness We All Share

As Patriots We'll Salute As It Rises
To The Anthem As It Begins To Play
Il Bandiera Ta Malta, We Shall Toast The Deceased
Rest In Peace, I Hope They May

It Stands For Our Freedom
For The Respect Of Its People
For The Sacrifice Of A Nation
No Gender Separates Us, We Are All Equal

Ill Bandiera Ta Malta, We Stand By It
Just A Piece Of Linen Textile
With A History So Rich And Pure
Won't You Read My Story, Perhaps Stay Awhile

Talk A Moment, Over Pastizzi And Kinnie
Learn More Of This Great Nation's Flag
Il Bandiera Ta Malta
I'll Honour It, Sorry, Don't Mean To Brag

For Bravery, This Flag Rightfully Issued
Came September 64, In Vibrant Colours
For Duties Beyond Their Call
Heeding The Calls Of The Sisters And Brothers

When Next You See This Flag In The Breeze
Embrace The Courage, Which Men, Women Gained
And Gave, This Island Of Malta Though Small
Heroism, To This Day, Still Remained

THE FIRE OF DESTRUCTION

Since Men First Laid Foot On This Earth
Waging War Against Their Brother
Their Homes Burning To The Ground
With No Money To Buy Another

That Fire Which Left Us Bare
No Money To Our Name
Cept The Shirt Upon Our Back
And No One Will Take The Blame

The Fire Of Destruction
Consuming All That's Around
Where Nothing Will Ever Survive
Till Nothing Will Be Ever Found

All Around Me Fire Burning
An Explosion Shot Into Blaze
People Scampering, Bodies Flying
Perhaps These Are The End Of Days

The Air Reeked Of Decomposing Flesh
Suchlike The Stench Of A Rotting Corpse
That Woken From An Egyptian Tomb
As If Like Some Theatrical Props

They Cried For Freedom
But Salvation Was Never At Hand
In Every Direction People On Their Knees Prayed
And Hoped They Would Not Be Damned

We Waited For The Rains
To Soothe Away The Fire Of Destruction,
But All Around, Prayers Unanswered
And That Maybe, All This, Was A Deception

I Feared There Would Be No Ending
The Skies Turned A Crimson Red That Night
As The Moon Hid Behind The Smokey Clouds
And All Around, The Land Was Devoid Of Light

Ashes Flickered Beneath The Street Lamps
As They Sailed Into The Breeze
Like Moths To A Flame
They Fluttered With Ease

Raindrops, From The Sky Scattered
"Perhaps Our Prayers Were Answered"
I Heard One Lady Cry Out
As People All Around Looked Skyward, Gathered

The Fire Of Destruction
A Price We Nearly Came To Pay
It Was History Repeating Itself
And Those Memories Shan't Ever Go Away

SHADOWS IN THE FLAME

In The Night, When The Stillness Stirs
There's Only The Silence That It Gathered
But All That Remains, The Softened Breeze
And No Murmur's Ever Heard

Shadows In The Flame
That Are Concealed Behind, What Is True
Dancing Like Ripples Coming In And Out
Never Coming Into Full View

Like Shadows Casting Illusion
The Truth, Casts No Lies
We Live In World Of Make Believe
But Hide Amidst An Impenetrable Disguise

Shadows In The Flame That Lurk,
Following Closely Behind
They Are A Deception Of Reality
But In Our Minds, We Are Confined

Like The Shadows Concealed
Undisturbed By The Light
Creeping, Slithering On By
Blending With The Night

Like Shadows, That Diminish
So Are The Memories That We've Sustained,
Discarded Along The Way
Those Moment, We Treasured And Pained

Like The Shadows In The Flame
Those We Have Come To Forget
Leaving A Reminder What The Past Once Held
We Paid Our Dues, Paid Our Debts

In Darkness, No Shadows Be Cast
No Silhouettes, Just Light Devoid
What Once Held Life
Now, Everything We Valued Has Been Destroyed

HOPE I DIDN'T WAKE YOU

You were looking sound asleep

I didn't want to wake

You

But something's been

Playing on my

Mind

How we never talk, days

On end, if only you

Knew

But to tell you, how could

I tell you, the words

I couldn't

Find

Sleepless nights, tossed

And turned, the early

Morning hours crept

In

I needed to tell you

Something, but thought

How

Your eyes wide open

Beside me, now's a good time

Anxiety building up

Within

My mouth gaped open
But no words would
allow

honey! I've something

important to tell you

something, may make you

proud

I am pregnant with your

Child, a child to calls
Ours

I did the test, and I

Have only just

Found

Kept wanting to tell you

Slept on it, all night for

hours

"I hope you're not mad,

But thought you should

Know"

"I cannot be more excited

That we are now a

Family"

"a son, a daughter, gorgeous

I'm sure they will

Grow"

Eyes of blue with a heaven smile
To that, just have to wait and
See

THE DEMONS WITHIN

You Can't See Them, But They're There
Lurking Inside, Controlling Your Thoughts
I Don't Know What To Believe Anymore
Tried To Find Help, The Many Times I've Sought

The Demons Within, Dwell In My Mind's Crevices
How Can I Confront, Come Face To Face
When I Don't Even Know Who I Am
Or How To Find Grace

How Can I Find The Strength Within
To Overcome My Fears
When I Struggle With The Challenges Of Life
That Come My Way When Suddenly They Appear

I Will Not Walk Away, But Will Stand Tall
Take A Hold Of Who I Am, Or What I'll Be
I Don't Know, How Or What I Feel
Only That, I Want To Be Free

My Actions, I Have To Suffer Their Consequences
My Flaws, And There Are Many
I Must Try To Correct Them
And I Accept, There Are Plenty

I Have No Courage, To Accept Who I Am
No Sparks, Not A Flicker, To Set Me Alight
I'll Walk Away When I Get Scared
It's My Inner Demons That I Must Fight

I Do Not Dwell, On What I Don't Possess
No Fame, Power Or Pleasures
Only My Beliefs, In That I Could Be Someone
I Won't Live Up To Anyone's Measures

For It Is Hard To Rely Upon,
What I Cannot Yet Trust
When I Feel You Distancing Away
With Time I Will Learn To Adjust

I Feel The Demons From Within,
The Ghosts, I'll Do My Best To Hide
These Haunt Me As I Sleep
With Dreams, I Cannot Set Aside

I've Been Poisoned By The Demons Within
Filled With Doubts And False Ideals
I Have Suffered from the Worries And Fear
It's My Heart, They Have Tried To Steal

I Know I Will Survive These Battles
That For So Long Have Had To Concede
There Are No Promises, To Achieve These Dreams
Yet It Is The Assurance That I Will Need

I Will Triumph Over My Inner Demons
When In Myself I Have Come To Believe
It Is Then I Will Find Peace
And Peace Of Mind I Will Receive

WALK AWAY

When Troubles In My Life Drags Me To Despair
The Anger Tells Me To Attack
In Rage I Want So Much To Fight
But Walk Away And Never Look Back

Many Will Test You, But Believe In Self Worth
You Have The Strength To Walk Away,
The Courage To Rise Above Your Debtors
With Your Spirit To Show You The Way

It Doesn't Mean That You're Weak,
With Your Head Held High
Go Out And Show The World
Give Yourself A Chance, If Only You Try

Then The World Will See Your Wonder
Stand Up On Your Own Two Feet
And Shrug Off Their Disbelief
Your Life As Certain Will Be Complete

And Those That Jeered, Will Come To Admire
So Raise A Glass, Your Confidence Will Follow
At Times You Need To Just Walk Away
And Leave The World That Was, Also.

Have No Regrets Because Of Beliefs
It's Ok To Say No, When It Threatens This
Though Anger And Frustrations Can Defeat
Your Feelings, You Cannot Dismiss

It's The Better Man, They Say, That Walks Away
Doesn't Look Back In Disgrace
He Will Close The Door Behind Him
And Hope Ahead, Be A Better Place,

Away From The Hurt, Familiar Distrust
Keeps On Walking, Avoiding Conflicts
Listen To Your Heart, Walk Away From The Troubles
For Every Problem, He Thinks, There Is A Fix

Though The Road Ahead Be Jagged Edged
I Will Not Cry, Because I Have Fallen
Will Only Make Me Stronger
Listening To Those Inner Voice Calling

"Walk Away" They Keep Urging
Times I Cannot Tell What's Gone Wrong
Or If At All I Care, And Pretend All's Fine
Should I Say Good Bye, Coz Here, I Don't Belong

THE NEW ME

I've Been Lost In The Wilderness Of My Mind
But There, I Found Solace In The Things I Want
Learning To Stand Up For Myself
What I Believe, Or Perhaps What I Don't

I Found The New Me
In Crevices, Tiny Cracks In The Conscious Mind
There, No-One Will Approach
They Won't See Me, Or Ever Will Find

Who Is The New Me?
I Am Me, Myself And I, No Other In Between
Don't Expect Me To Conform
Comply, I Will Not, Just The Way I've Been

I May Not Live Up To Your Expectations
But That's Ok, Fine To Be Different
You Judge Me By My Actions And Words
Instead Of The Good Deeds, I Have Meant

I Bare The Labels Society Has Inflicted
My Character They Have Betrayed
Getting To Know The New Me
And The Sacrifices I Have Made

In A World Of Fighting, Being Rejected
Kept Struggling To Keep Alive
I Knocked On Your Door, Upon Me, You Closed
My Head Above Water, Just To Survive

You Punish, What You Don't Understand
Confined, Chained And Constricted
You Disliked The New Me
And Barred Me Away, Like A Criminal Convicted

I Fought Your Hatred, Your Scrutiny
Your Critical Put Down
Took Anything I Would Call Mine
And Upon My Head, Placed A Thorned Crown

My Name, What Is It?
Many Times I Cannot Recall
You Have Stripped From Me, My Identity
This Burden, I Have Come To Haul

I Was Only Seeking Salvation
Redemption I Could Not Receive
Cried Out, But Not One Listened
I Guess, In Me, You Could Not Believe

I Won't Bow Down To My Enemies
Nor Ask For Forgiveness
My Opinions, To Always Will Voice
I Know Will Be Persecuted For This

The New Me, I Cannot Find Shame
This Person, I Was Destined To Be
Many Egg Shells Have Come To Be Broken
Watching Over My Shoulder To Be Free

I Have Been Enslaved By My Captors
No Chains Did Ever Hold Me Down
This World Will Again Welcome Me
Walking The Streets In A Kings Royal Gown

THE DREAMS I PROMISED YOU

I Wanted To Give You The World
But In The End, Gave You
Nothing
I Was Laid Off, Jobs Were Scarce
Barely Enough On The
Table
We Had Mouths To Feed
Rent Too Was Rarely
Paid
The Dreams I Promised You
Nothing More Than Fairytales
May Never Be
Coming
But Will Try My Hardest
The Best I Can, That, If Im
Able
To Live Up to The Promises
To You I
Made
The Dreams I Promised You
My Dear, One Day, You'll
See
You Won't Need Wealth, A Mansion
Or Fame, You Have Me, What Really
Matters

Together Hand In Hand, To

Rise Above

Despair

We Can Live In A House, A House

We'll Call Our Own. It's How Its Gonna

Be

Will Make Our Dreams Come Real

I Pray They Won't Be

Shattered

In This World, Where Everything

We Have, We Will

Share

Some May Say That Im A Fool

Some Might Even Call Me

Crazy

But If We Dream All

Will Seem To Be Very

Possible

The Dreams I Promise You

Are A Vision What I Believe Is

True

All That I Ask, All That I Need

To Trust In Me

Baby

When I Have You By My Side
When I Know You Believe
We Can Dodge Any
Obstacles
And Any Challenges We
Are To Be Put
Through

AS I STOP TO COUNT MY BLESSINGS

As I Stop To Count My Blessings
There Is One Thing Which Rings True
I'll Always Be So Grateful
For The Friend I Found In You

Grateful For The Special Times
We've Shared Through The Years
Times That Brought Us Closer
Through Our Laughter And Our Tears

Grateful Just To Have Someone
As Kind And Good As You
To Share My Finest Moments With
And Share My Sorrows Too

And When I Look Upon My Life
What Matters In The End
Is That I Was Really Lucky
To Find One, True Faithful Friend

As I Stop To Count My Blessing
One Thing That Rings True
I'm Grateful For A Friend, I Found In You

For The Special Times, Through The Years
Bringing us closer through the
Laughter and the tears

Grateful To Have Someone, So Kind
And Wonderful As You
Sharing moments. The joys and sorrows too

When I Look Upon My Life, What Matters
The Most In The End,
Is That I Found My Faithful Friend

IN THE DEPTH OF NOTHINGNESS

I Find Myself Falling Deeper And Deeper
Into A Dark And Depthless Abyss
Not A Hint Of Light, Just A Void, Empty And Hollow
There Is Nothing To See In All This

There Is Only Peace And Tranquillity
Down Here Below, I Can Feel No Pain
Merely, The Solitude And Silence Undisturbed
In The Depth Of Nothingness, Stillness Remains

No One Can Hear Your Screams
In This Blackened Chasm
Where Dangers May Lurk
Beneath You, The Deeper Down You Fathom

In The Depth Of Nothingness
There's A Cold And Eerie Chill
My Body, Immersed In Coldness
Then Suddenly From Nowhere, A Deafening Shrill

As My Body Floats In Numbness
Motionless To Conserve My Breathing
By Now Becoming Shallow
Gotta Keep Moving, To Prevent My Heart Not Beating

In The Depth Of Nothingness
Where This Darkness Yields No Life
What Am I Doing Here
I Cannot Quite Define

In The Deafening Silence
Surely Something Must Exist
No Light Nor Even Shadows
What Perils Have Come To Lie In The Midst

All I Can See, An Endless Sea Of Empty Space
In The Depth Of Nothingness
Where Time Ceases To Thrive
And All Around Me, Nothing But Emptiness

Drifting Weightless, Like A Man In Space
Above Him, Below Him Only Stars Do Shine
That Glitter In Their Radiance
And Together, Constellations Align

In The Depth Of Nothingness
Where The Cold And Deep, Banishes The Warmth
As The Vastness Consumes It All
And There Solitude Is Formed

In The Boundless Expanse Of The Depths Below
Dreams Dissolve And Hopes Shattered
And Existence Ceases To Be
Then Our Thoughts Become Slowly Scattered

What Looms Beneath The Depth Of Nothingness
An Infinite Realm Into A Vast Void
Where Not Even Light Penetrates
And No Vessel Had Ever Spoiled

In That Intense And Endless Deep
Forever, One Might Travel Into This Bottomless Pit
Never To Reach Destination Point
So Poorly And Dimly Lit

In The Silence That Echoes
My Head Becoming Weary
Vision With The Growth Of Fatigue
My Eyes, Upon Emptiness, Cannot See Clearly

I Will Ascend Now
From The Depths Of Nothingness
Where Peace Has Comforted Me
From Down, Miles Below The Surface

ASTRAL PLAINS

Oceans Apart In A Far Distant Plain
Separated By Time And
Space
All Around, Just Emptiness
And Wondering If Anything Really
Exists
In My Mind, To Go
Where Angels Dance On Air
If Only There's Such A
Place
Yearning To Hold You In This
Dream Like State, If Only God
Permits
Motionless, In My Bed, Hypnagogia
Visions Of Half
Asleep
Not Yet Awake, In A Body
Not Fully
Aware
Drifting, Wondering Where
I'm Going, Or If My Spirit I Will
Release
Nothing In Front Of Me
Nothing At All, Hazy, Just A
Blur

Aimlessly Floating, Feels
So Right, Feel So At
Peace
I Know You're There, Though
I Can't Find
You
From Above The Clouds, Beyond
This Sphere, I Must
Explore
I Must Get To You, But Many
Mountains Between,
This Splendour
View
Too High To Ascend, But
Into The Outer Cosmos I Must
Soar
I Feel My Spirit In The Astral Plain,
Projecting, Beneath Me,
My Body Lies
Still
Am I Living In A Sleep Like Reality
A Utopian
Dream
In A New World, Within A
Different Dimension
No Warmth, Feel The
Chill

You Cannot Be Heard,

Sound Is Void, Empty,

Though You May

Scream

Higher Into The Plains

I Astral, Before Me,

Colours In

Array

The Blues And Greens, Orange

And Red

Collide

Swirling, Sidewinding Across

The Sky, Into Where The Night

Meets The

Day

In A Distance An Astral Image,

I Cannot See, Though

The Many Ways I

Tried

It Approaches Me In

A Similar Body, Guided By Its Silver

Cord

Your Body Nears Me

Your Guiding Hand I

Take

In An Brief Instance, We
Are One Body
Transformed
I Knew Then, When Two Worlds
Unite, You And I, Were No
Mistake
Our Transparent Bodies
Dance As One, Cords
Intertwined
This Moment Of Togetherness
No One Could Take
Away
I've Known What I Wanted
Long Before. It Is
Your Name Upon My Heart I've
Signed
One Day From Our Spirits
To Our Bodies, We'll Be Together I
Pray
Our Bodies In Tune
Drifting Off In The Nightly Mist,
No Presence Of
Time
Just You And I, Not A Care
In This Plain, Only This Moment Lasts
Forever

I Know Deep Within I'll
Find You, And That
Those Mountains Will Have
Climbed
Until That Day That I Do
I'll Continue To Search Won't Give Up
Never

THE CLAIRVOYANT

Sitting At A Table At Some Fairground Attraction
Dressed In A Silky Gown, To Play His Mystic Role
The Clairvoyant Delves In The Psychic Realm
Before Long, Looking Deep Into Your Soul

He Shuffles His Tarot Deck Of Cards
Announcing His Price For The Read
With His Heightened Senses
He Fans A Spread

Asking You To Select Four Cards
But To Have A Question In Mind
With His Eyes Closed, Begins To Meditate
To Contact His Spirit Guide

In A Trance Like State Of Mind
His Body, Uncontrolled, Begins To Shake
Your Laughter, Though You Try, You Cannot Control
Concentration Broken, A Restart He Must Make

Telling You It Is Serious Business
Needing To Be In Full Focus, Dealing With The Spirit World
You Comply With His Request, So Then Continues
When Voices, In His Head Emerged

From Beyond The Grave, The Paranormal Realm
Visions Of "Those Around Him" Come Through
In His Mind, Flashes Of Light
With Suspense, My Anxiety Grew

I Listened With Intent, As Messages
From The Other Side, Were Relayed
I Used To Question With Disbelief
Now Curiosity On My Mind, Weighed

An Hour Had Passed, Still The Clairvoyant,
His Perceptive Powers He Unleashed
Secrets Of My Life, That Only I Knew
And Family, Long Gone, Now Deceased

I Was Never One To Explore The Supernatural
Research Or Least Of All, My Interest In The Occult
Not Even In The Magical World, As A Kid
But Always Questioned, As An Adult

A Catholic Growing Boy, Was Always
Told Never To Believe In That Stuff
But Prophecies In The Bible, I Was Told Do Exist
I Was Asked To Be Quiet, And That Was Enough

So, I Grew Up, Very Curious Minded
Just Had To See, To Just Believe
The Clairvoyant, With His ESP, Helped To Understand
That Greater Powers, Can Be Received

With A Clear Vision, No Fake Crystal Ball
Just Looking With His Third Eye
I Paid For His Flawless Insight
As I walked away, saying good-bye

PSYCHIC REALM

The Moon, The Star, Universal Galaxies
The Planetary Spheres
Within This Vast And Endless Plain,
Man Will Travel To Reach Boundless Frontiers

Will Enter Into The Psychic Realm
Beyond What We Conceive Or Imagine Real
To Delve And Search By Any Means
A Journey To Venture Into The Surreal

By The Power Of The Mind
In A Comatose Like State
Dimmed Breath, Lying Upon His Bed
He Astral Projects By Chance Or A Twist Of Fate

His Quest Into The Unknown
Lies Before Him, Like An Web Weaved
With Oddities And Fascination
Reality Is Never As It Seemed

Into The Psychic Realm
Tarot Readers With Angel, Oracle Cards
Mesmerising To Thrill With Their Witchery
Being Cautious, Keeping Their Guards

For The Would-Be Sceptic
Scrutinises Their Every Move
But Listens Attentively
Trying Hard To Disprove

In The Psychic Realm
Clairvoyants With A Crystal Ball
Upon Which Light Through It Shines
Awaits His Spirit's Call

A Protection Prayer Before Starting
Cleanses The Air To Meditate
"Is Anyone Present, Wishing To Come Through"
Summons The Spirits, In A Corner A Ball Levitates

A Scream, Hairs Standing On End
Startled With Fright
The Room Ignites "Is That You John"
As The Reading Continues Into The Night

Back And Forward, Commuting
From The Other Side
Messages From Beyond The Grave
From Those Who Have Died

Deceased, Perhaps Not Long Ago
Be A Friend, A Wife, Or A Mother,
A Distant Relative Or Husband
Wanting To Be At Peace With Another

Channelling His Energy
Awaits From Those Crossed Over
The Room Stares In Silence. A Pinch
Of Dread Upon Their Faces Draws Closer

In The Psychic Realm
Where Mystics Dwell
And Empaths Roam The World
All With Readings In The Ability To Foretell

Healing Hands Placed Upon You
Many Of Which Do Exist
Palmistry, Reiki And Massage
In Your Health Will Assist

Pendulum And Divining Rods
To Answer The Yes And No
Perhaps Seen As An Illusion
But How Are We Really To Know

In The Psychic Realm
Where Auras Draw On Your Emotions
With The Rainbow Spectrum Of Colours
Your Mood Changes Begin To Open

In The Psychic Realm Where
Many Can Visualise What Isn't There
Be It A Spectre, A Ghost Or An Angel
All Just To Make You Aware

A DREAM OF THEIR OWN

Young At Heart, Their Lives
United And Pledged To Tie The Knot
With Vows, Spoken, Before God's Grace
Shared A Love, And Before Him, Was Brought

They'll Build A Dream Of Their Own
As The Many Before Them Had
Parents And Their Ancestors
Taking Each Other's' Hands

To Travel To A World Of Fantasy
Where Nothing Seems Impossible
Here, To Build A Dream Of Their Own
And Everything's Made Possible

A Blessing From Heaven
To Follow Their Dreams
These Are No Illusion
But In Reality, How Their Future Gleams

Will Grow Old Together
Making The Memories
That They Can Look Back On
That'll Lasts Throughout The Centuries

They Only Need Each Other
To Build These Dreams Of Their Own
And She'd Be His Queen
Along With Him On His Throne

They'd Only Have Each Other
To Live Their Lives Through
Run Away To Leave This World Behind
To A Brighter World That's New

They Will Build A Dream
Where Flowers Blossom The Year Round
And Here Wishes Come True
Where Oh Where, Can Such A Place Be Found

No Shadows Will Be Cast
No Hatred Dispersed Upon This Land
In This Vision, Only Love Prevails
Where Hatred And Malice, They Can Withstand

And Build A Home, Upon The Hills
Perhaps Near The Beach
To See Beyond The Horizon
Neath The Stars, Where The Imagination Can Reach

A Dream Of Their Own
Children Running Around In The Yard
Chasing Balls, Barking Dogs, And
Upon The Dirt, Their Names, And A Love Heart Carved

Dreams Are Short Lived
Then Reality Sets In
The World, Back To The Way It Was
To A Time, As It Was Back When

FLYING 30,000 FEET

Clouds Above Me, Clouds Below

Flying Through Mist, Far

As The Eye Can

See

In A Distance, The Sun Rises

Rays Creeping Across Clouds.

Blinded, But Admiring The

View

The Ocean From Above, Dolphins,

Like Specks, As They Skim The

Surface

What If I, Like Those Dolphins

Swim, Swimming Wild, Swimming

Free

Passing Ripples And Tides

Across The Vast Expanse Of

Blue

Flying 30,000 Feet, From Above

So Peaceful, Who Am I To Deserve

This

Solar Rays, Over The Horizon

Shines Its Tentacles Of

Light

The Sky, Changing Colours

Variants Shades Of Reds, Blues

And Ever-Changing

Hues

A Photo Moment, No

One Will Ever

Believe

Before My Eyes, In Awe

And Wonderment Of This Heavenly

Splendour At This

Sight

Moments Of Glory, Slowly Lost

A New Day Upon Me, This Sight

I Must Now

Lose

Will Be Back Another Day

And Upon Many, They Too, Will

Receive

"Turbulence", Flying At 30,000 Feet

Over The Speakers

Come

"No Cause For Alarm, Please

Remain Seated, Just Minutes

More"

Outside My Window, What Was

A Grandeur View, Now In A Darkened

Gloom

Thunder, Cracks Across The Sky
Rolls Like Some Tribal
Drum
Summoning Villagers To
Prepare For A Raging
War
Seat Buckled, Frightened
Shaking, And In Terror I Was
Consumed
Seatbelt Sign Off, The Light
Once More Gleamed
Through
A Sigh Of Relief, My
Discomfort Gently
Lifted
As The White Clouds Below
Painted The
Sky
Like A Painter's Brush
About To Depict A Scenic
View
Catching Each Moment Before
This Was Lost Or Ever
Drifted
Flying At 30,000 Feet, So
Much To Catch The
Eye

The Sun Comes Over The Skyline
The Day Has Breathed Its
Last
Deadness Below, The Waves
Sparkly Glimmer From The Distant
Moon
Before Long The Stilled Night
Draws Its Curtain, A New Day
Awaits
All Around Me, Visions Of Delight, Like
Heaven On Earth, Immensely
Vast
Flying 30,000 Feet, The Chilled
Wind, Like The Cold Winds Of
June
I Know My Journey Draws A
Close, I Look Towards Family
Who Down Below Will
Wait

YOU ARE MY SUNSHINE

"You Are My Sunshine", I Recall
Those Words Fondly
That My Momma Used To Sing For Me
Her Face, Her Words, Remembering Vividly

As If It Was Only Just Yesterday
When She'd Tuck Me Into Bed
With A Good Night Kiss
And Attentive, I Was, As She Read

Patiently, A Fairy Book Story
She Would Smile As She Left The Room
The Lights Turned Down Low
In That Instance, Her Love I Would Consume

Those Days Have Sadly Disappeared
But Her Memories Live Inside Of Me
And So Will That Song
And Hope, From It, Will Never Be Freed

The Years Travelled Fast
And So Was I Getting Older
I Met A Girl And Fell In Love
With Kids I'd Carry Upon My Shoulder

Bedtime Was A Special Time
Each Night, To Them, A Song I Sang
My Mother's Song, It Came To Be
You Are My Sunshine, These Words In My Head Rang

Indeed, They Were My Sunshine
The Reason I Wake Up Each Day Break
To Embrace The Dawn Of The Day
And A Hug, When My Children Will Awake

I Would Sing To Them
Those Same Words When Troubles Soared
Innocent Faces, Any Mother Would Adore
And Still My Love To Them Poured

The World Was Fine Again, At Peace
Never Forgetting What Children Mean
Until They Leave The Nest
To Never Upon You, Will They Lean

They've Made Me Happy
When The Clouds Became Grey
Till The Skies Once Again Opened Up
And Darkness Soon Drifted Away

They Were My Light In My Darkest Hours
My Strength When I Was Weak
When I Felt Down, They Were Besides Me
And My Voice When I Couldn't Speak

A Frown Upon My Face They Would See
"Are You Ok Daddy," The Youngest Would Say
But I Lied And Said Yes
He Smile And Carried On To Play

He Was Too Young To Understand
That One Day I Mayn't Be Here Much Longer
Every Day Was A Blessing, Lived As Was My Last
For Many Years I Watched Him Getting Stronger

As For Me, An Old Man
And To This Day, They Are Still My Sunshine
My Time Had Come, To Travel To The Beyond
To Be With My Maker, The Holy Divine

I Watch Over Them Now
From Beyond The Skies Of Blue
I Can Feel Them Looking Up At Me
When Every Day Is New

My Heart Still Sings That Very Tune
That Resonates Beyond The Pearly Heaven's Gates
Down Below My Children Now Smiling
And A Message From Me They Await

Looking Up To The Heavens
A Shooting Star Zipped Across The Night Sky
I See Them Making A Wish
That I Was There As My Youngest Darling, Did Cry

Clutching A Photo Of Me
Singing, You Are My Sunshine,
Heavenly Tears, Fell From My Eyes
I Could Not Hold Them, As I Did With Mine

Those Tears Became Raindrops Falling
Upon Their Tiny Face
On A Cloudy Summer's Day
If Only Just Awhile, To Hold Them For An Embrace

Even When They Become Old And Grey
I Was Always Their Sunshine
Every Day Of Their Lives
Forever And Always, Till The End Of Time

LETTING GO

We Were Married, Happily
Was How It All Started
I Was Dressed In White, Him By My Side
A Wedded Couple, But Years Later, Parted

He Was The Man Of My Dreams
Back When I Was Stupid And Naïve
Our Vows Were Taken Upon The Holy Book
Forever Lasting, I Came To Believe

A Life Together Like In Some Fairy Tale
But This Wasn't Such Story
Made Plans To Have Our Children
But Things Would Change, He Took Away The Glory

Lost His Job, Then Hit The Bottle
A Rage In Fisted Fury
Never Came Home, Days On End
And I Was To Blame, Never He

My Emotions Flowed That Instance
When I Had To Let Go
That Was The Journey I Had To End
What Was Installed For Me, I Had To Know

I Wanted Out, But How
Breaking Down In Tears
To Find A Way Of Letting Go
But Inside My Head, Circulating Fears

Letting Go Would Be The Hardest
Thing To Achieve
And I Would Welcome The Winds Of Change
But Firstly, The Confidence To Leave

I Stayed For My Children
In This Living Hell
Still Too Young To Understand
How It Feels, In This Prison Cell

He Stumbles Through The Door
Each And Every Night, Tattered Clothes
The Smell Of Liquor Upon His Breath
Where's He Been, God Only Knows

"Where's My Dinner"
In A Slurred Manner Of Speech
"Do You Know What Time It Is"
As For Another Bottle, He Tried To Reach

"Its 1am In The Morning
And The Kids Are Asleep"
His Anger Grew Stern
While My Patience I Had To Keep

Making Demands, To Which
I Would Not Comply
His Voice Escalating
Grabbed A Pistol, Looking Into My Eye

Raving, "I'll Shoot, I'll Shoot"
Waking The Kids Out Of Bed
"Go Back To Bed Honey"
"Please Listen To What I Said"

"Everything's Fine, Daddy's Just Tired"
With A Gun Against My Head,
Threatened To Pull The Trigger
If I'd Not Have Listened, Instead

Had To Do Something, And Quick
But What! My Mind In A State Of Alarm
And How Can I, A Meekly Woman
A Grown Man, Disarm

There Was No Escaping
Till The Phone, Upon The Wall Rang
Startled, He Cocked That Pistol
This Was My Chance, To My Feet I Sprang

This Was My Chance, Had To Get
The Children Out
I Pleaded For Our Lives, Battered, Bruised
Yelling, With A Might Shout

Run! Chord Tangled Around My Feet
Lunging For The Door
He Grabbed At My Skirt
As A Bullet Ricocheted To The Floor

I Had To Let Go, Start A New Life
There Was No Going Back
These Memories, I Had To Block Out
To Keep My Life On Track

Had To Let Go Of My Past
But Still My Future, Looked Grim
No Place To Call My Own
Now Being Deserted By Him

A Weight That's Been Lifted, Long Have I Carried
Finally Came Crashing
This Burden That Would Remind Me
Of The Struggles, Came Before Me Flashing

Those Memories Of Yesteryears
Echo With Torment, And In My Mind, Have Stayed
But Like Any Memory,
They Too, Would Soon Come To Fade

A Life Of Destitution, Nowhere To Run
A Voice Inside My Head "A Time For Letting Go"
"Get Up, Move On" Telling Myself
I Was Prepared For What Life Would Throw

Stepping Into The Unknown
Nothing To Lose But Gain
Ahead, A Beacon Of Light, That Lit The Way,
Away From The Solitude, Where I Would Not Remain

Letting Go, I Welcomed The Peace
That My Heart, For So Long Had Missed
A Gentle Hand Guided Me Through
Knowing Somewhere In This World, Love Exists

GOOD MORNING BEAUTIFUL

You Were Resting, Sound Asleep

Eyes Shut

Tight

I Didn't Wanna Wake You

Seeing You Lying

There

My Hand Upon Your Chest

As You Exhaled

Inhaled

I Wanted To Wake You

But Didn't Turn On The

Light

Caressed You Gently, Ran My

Fingers Through Your

Hair

Your Golden Strands, Gleaming

A Smile Upon My Face, This Never

Failed

Your Eyes Glimpsed Mine

"Good Morning Beautiful"

How Did You

Sleep

Your Arms Stretched Out

Your Body

Contoured

I Want To Lay Besides You

My Body Wrapped In

Yours

When I See Your Smile

It's You I Want To

Keep

I Would Make This Day Last

Forever, If Only I

Could

Wanting You So Much

So Much, Like Never

Before

Good Morning Beautiful

Can't Tell You Enough, How Much You've

Meant

Lying Here, Body To Body, I

Shan't Waste This Day

Away

If I Could Make A Wish,

A Wish, You'd Never Have To

Leave

I Think Of The Heavens

And It's You, To Me, They've

Sent

A While Longer, Please
I'll Beg You To
Stay
You Have Given Me Hope
In Someone That I Can
Believe
Good Morning Beautiful
How Did You
Sleep

DISTANCE

Lakes And Rivers, Mountains
And The Plain
The Distance May Divide Us,
But Our Love Will Never Wane

Even If The Space Seems So Remote
Only Time Will Stand Between Us
Just How Will I Get To You
I Will Find A Way, This You Can Trust

Over The Horizon, I Must Journey
If I, To Ever See You Again
Your Voice, I Hear You Calling
Beyond Expanse Of Water, That Extends

However, The Distance Between Us grows
You're Only A Thought Away
Close, As The Sun To The Light
And The Night To The Day

One Without The Other
Is Like A Heaven Without Our God
Or Warmth To Remedy The Cold
Just As You And I, Have That Special Bond

I Feel Imprisoned, Confined, By This Distance
Like Bars, I Cannot Penetrate
And Only You Can Open, If I, To See You Again
To Lift Off This Burden, This Weight

Although The Distance Between, May Be Vast
We Will Always Be Connected
One Body, One Mind, One Spirit
Our Love Will Never Be Tested

I Want My Life To Revolve Around You
Every Waking Hour, And In My Dreams
I'd Travel To The Moon, The Stars
In The Bleak Of Weather, In All Extremes

The Cosmos, Galaxies Will Not Be Far Enough
I'll Tell You Darling, Will Get To You, This I Know
No Matter How Distanced Away
My Promise I Will Keep, And Will Show

Love Has No Bounds, Has No Limits
Whether You're Close, Or Vastly Separated
I Can Feel You Near Me
My Affection For You, Has Never Faded

Longing To Touch, Feel, Hear You
To Savour Each And Every Second
But How Can I, So Far Apart We're Spread
I Must Keep My Doubts At Bay, Distant

I Want To Leave This Reality
So Far From Me, Behind
And Live Within My Dreams
Where My Hopes And Promises, Will Not Decline

THE BOND

Barely Minutes Old, And Out Of
The Womb, First Sounds Of
Crying

Scrunched Up Face, Eyes
Exploring, To Feel His Mother's
Touch

Her Soft Tender Skin Nestles
Against His Head, Making His Way To
Feed

The Bond Between Mother And Son
In The Instance Of Birth, Is A Love
Undying

That No Mother Could Love
Her Child, Generously As
Much

Since The Day Of Conception,
When In The Womb, Was Planted A
Seed

She Marvels At Her Creation
Nine Months In The
Making

That Special Bond, Which Cannot
Be Cut, Never
Severed

As She Caresses His Head
And Upon It, A
Kiss

That Baby Child, New To This World,

Suckling, With Every Breath

Taking

A Face Of Wonder, A Miracle

Took Place, Priceless, That Cannot Be

Measured

Bringing Up A Life, An Experience

No Woman To

Miss

The Bond That Cannot Be Broken,

His Blood Runs With

Hers

Mother And Child, This Angelic

Face She

Stares

A Tear, Trickles Down Her Cheek

Slowly Wiping

Away

Soft And Gentle, Body Wrinkled

Lies Quietly, Not

Stirred

A Healthy Being, God Has Given

Thankful To The Answered

Prayers

Taking In The Moments,

Taking In The Scene, To Relish In This

Day

SOME NIGHTS

Some Nights I Wonder

What It Is You Are

Doing

Alone In My Bed

Restless Sleeps And Wishing I Was

There

You Cannot Know My Feelings

And Thinking, It's You I May Be

Losing

I Want To Ring You, But

Don't Wanna Wake You

To Remedy My

Despair

Some Nights I Wonder

If At All You Really

Cared

Took Me For Granted,

And Thought I Would Never

Leave

Can't Make It On My Own

Too Much To Let Go

Too Much We Have

Shared

We Could Make It Together
If Both Of Us Came To
Believe
Some Nights I Wake Up
I Vision You Beside
Me
Are U Really Here
Or Am I Just In A Dream
Land
Cause There I Know
Only Way I Can Be
Free
I Reach Out To Touch You
But Disappear, Leaving You
Was Never
Planned
Some Nights Are Lonely
Darling, You Cannot
Imagine
I Read Letters You've Sent,
Memorise Your Picture,
Ingrained In My
Dreams
Each Night I Lay And Ponder
How Did This
Happen

No Answers, No Conclusion

Cannot Explain How Much You

Mean

Some Nights I Pray For An

Ending, Just Hope You Return

Home

But I Know The Phone

Won't Ring, Nor Messages

Sent

Had You Always Planned

To Let Me Perish, Gave Me Up To

Roam

Leaving Me To Wonder, Who I Was,

To Be, Or Who I Am, When You

Left

RAGE AND FURY

When You've Had Enough
Let The World Pass
By
It's Too Late To Make
Amends With Nothing Left To
Say
Your Promises, Your Lies
I Trusted In You, But Bled Me
Dry
How Can We Go On When
You Don't Care, Departing This
Way
You Said You Loved Me
But Did You Really
Care
You're Never Here For
Me, I Was Left In
Tatters
Stranded, on the highway,
Just Left Me
There
I Guess, To You
Nothing Really
Matters
Leaving Me Behind
When I Depended On
You

And Played Me Like A Fool
Your Jack In The
Box
How Can I Believe All
You Had Said, Be
True
When Your Lies And
Deceptions Never
Stops
When You Look In The Mirror
Do You Hate What You've
Become?
An Image Of Distortion
Blemished From The
Truth
Return To The Pits Of
Hell, Or Wherever You Came
From
Share With Others, Who've
Lived Life By The
Untruth…
I Don't Care What Our Future
Holds, Coz Ain't No
Us
I Know In Time That,
You Will, From My Memory
Pass

To Carry On With My Life
And Learn To
Adjust
Then Truly Will I Know
My Pains I'd Have
Surpassed
Do You Recall I Drove My
Chevy Through Your
Door
You Never Came,
Of Reasons You Weren't
Home
In Rage And Anger, Determined
To Settle The
Score
A Note From Your Mother
Said You Weren't On Your
Own
Had Left This Town
On The Next Train
Out
With Rage And Fury,
Its Fire Burnt From
Within
Told Me In A Softly
Spoken Voice, "It's You
He Can Do
Without"

She Continued To Say
"His Love You Cannot
Win"
Recalling The Night
He Drove You To My
Place
I Saw You Kiss Him From
My Window That
Night
Waited For My Problems
To Dissolve, But All I Could
See Was Your
Face
In A Silhouetted Image
From The Lamppost
Light
Filled With Regrets,
Had We Never Met, My Life Would Be
Bliss
Your Lies And Deceit
My Trust You Had
Taken
I'll Be Over You When You
Are Gone, Not
Someone I Would
Miss

If You're Think I'm Wrong
You Are Gravely
Mistaken
Rage And Fury, You
Lied, Said You Were
Working
I Picked Up The Phone
But, Not To Be
There
Was Sure You Said
You'll Be Late, This, I Was
Certain
My Mind Kept Wondering
"She's Having An
Affair-"
Many Times I Rang You
Said To Leave A
Message
I Had Waited For Hours
But Never A
Call
I Have Accepted Your
Departure, Perhaps It's Just A
Blessing
No Memories Of You
Have I Left To
Recall

WHILE THE WORLD SLEEPS

Darkness Sets Across The Nation
Every Country Every Land
Stars At Midnight, Losing Their Dazzled Shimmer
And Still The Night Expands

Satellites, Upon Their Axis, Turning
While The World Sleeps And Wander,
Dreaming, Perhaps Never To Awaken
From Their Weary, Unbroken Slumber

While The World Sleeps
One By One, The Lights Phase Out
As The Night Slowly Eats The Day Away
Across The Miles, The World, Throughout

Sounds, Barely Heard, If At All
Only The Deafening Echoes Of Silence
Over And Over The Miles
Across The Vast Distance

While The World Sleeps
Time Stands Still Upon The Ticking Clocks
You Fight To Get Up, But Cant
Leaves Your Body In A State Of Shock

There Is A Sense Of Calmness
But Not Awake To Enjoy
Tranquillity Could Be A Permanent Thing
Not That We'll Have A Choice

While The World Sleeps
At The Mercy Of God,
By His Hands, Can We Ever See The Day Again
If Light, Upon This Earth Ever Poured

Silence, Rules Over, In The Depth Of Night
No Movement, Nor The Wind Did Stir
While The World Sleeps
There Seems No Reprieve At Hand, Near

What Once Started From A Grain Of Sand,
Or A Thought, In This Created World
This Planet With Flora And Fauna
Into Hyper Space, May Be Hurled

While The World Sleeps And Drifting Away
When The Sight Grows Bleak,
And Blindness, Upon Us Falls
It Will Be A Righteous Pardoning, That We'll Seek

We Are Hounded By The Night
Drifting Into A Deep Sleep
Into The Chasms Of Our Minds
There Dreams Set In, And Slowly They Creep

When The World Awakens
From What Might Have Been An Eternal Rest
Will They Know, Was Just A Dream
Or Were Their Beliefs, Just Put To A Test

Were Dreams, Merely a Disguise,
to Hide illusions From The Truth
and Camouflage The Here And Now
To Determine The Outcome, From What We Choose

While The World Slept
Scars Were Left Behind
Scars, From The Present And The Past
That In Our Minds, Were Left Confined

We Woke As If Nothing Ever Happened
It Was Only An Illusion, A Fantasy
While The World Did Sleep
We Escaped From A Virtual Reality

YOU ARE THE REASON

When I Go To Bed At Night
I Know A Day Will Soon To
Follow
You're The Reason, The Sun Rises.
That Brightens Up My
Day
You're My Every Thought,
My Every Vision, When I Think Of
You
Nothing Can Ever Replace
Your Smile, Or When Your Eyes
Glow
They'll Glisten, Touched By The Light,
Reflecting Its Colours
Array
Shades Of Reds, Blues, Yellows
And All The Rainbow
Hues
You're The Reason My Heart So Aches,
I Miss Your Presence, The Kiss Upon My
Lips
Want My Arms Around You, The Further
From Me You
Are
Only Your Painted Picture In My Mind
The Contours Of Your Face, I Cannot
Feel

It's Like Something Within Has Died
Like Something Within's Been
Ripped
I Will Get To You Somehow
No Matter How
Far
Will Swim The Oceans Vast, And The
Heavens I'll Soar, To you Then, My Love shall
Reveal
You're The Reason I Believe
In The Miracles Of Our Lives'
Story
In The Miracles Of You, Me,
Together As
One
Me Without You, Is Like An
Ocean Without Fish, A Sister Without A
Brother
United, We Can Build A Life,
Filled With All Its
Glory
We Will Cherish And Inspire,
It's Our Hearts, We Will Have
Won
Through The Paths We Travel
To Defend And Treasure Each
Other

MIRACLES DO COME TRUE

A Blind Man To See From

Once A Life Of

Darkness

A Crippled Soldier To Walk

Again From Upon The Battled

Fields

Miracles Do Come True,

Each Day The Light Of A Brand

New Day, Moves From The

Blackness

A Baby Cries Into This World

First Breaths, Comforted

As Its Mothers

Shields

Miracles Do Come True,

The Rain Falling, When The

Heavens Will

Cry

Or The Stars That Glistens,

Will Shine Upon Our

Sphere

We Accept It, But

Never Really Ever Wonder

Why

Life, Taken For Granted, Here

One Day, Then Finally To
Disappear

The Wind Upon Your Face

A Flower At Our Tender
Touch

So Frail At The Hands Of

Nature That Surrounds With
Beauty

Its Vast Splendour, Its

Grandeur Promises So
Much

Miracles Do Come True

If You Only But Look, If You
Only But
See

Miracles Are Around Us

From The Time Of Waking

Till The Sun Goes
Down

People Amongst Us, Many
We Do Not
Know

A Friendly Shoulder To

Cry On, Or Someone To Be
Around

To Pick You, When In Dark
Despair Or A Time Of Feeling
Low

Miracles Do Come True
If You Only But
Notice

You Might Not Walk On

Water, Turn Water Into

Wine

Miracles, Around Us, The Birth

Of A Child, From A Growing

Foetus

These Things We Call Miracles

At Time So Hard To

Define

We sustain life, at times

Do take it

Away

Miracles Do Come True

A Tear From Our Eyes, A Smile

From Our

Lips

Ever Stopped To Wonder

The Majesty Of Life, Or

Perhaps God's Natural

Way

Look All Around You, Marvel

God's Creation, From The

Seas Below To The Earth Total
Eclipse
Miracles Do Come True.

UNSPOKEN

As I Scribbled Into The Air
The Words I Found To Be Unspoken
These Were What I Longed To Say
But In My Mind, Were Broken

When At Times I Fumbled,
My Thoughts To Speak, Just Scattered
Just How To Show I Cared
When Mere Words I Nervously Stuttered

Never Shared My Feelings, Those, The Unspoken
Could Never Achieve All That Is Meant
No Thoughts To Say "I Love You"
These, That Are Only Dreamt

Only A Smile Or A Troubled Frown
Can Replace The Unspoken Word
A Teardrop, To Let You Know I Care
And That I Miss You, This In My Mind, Stirred

Unspoken, Were The Words
I could Never Convey That I Was Sorry
I Was Drowning In My Self Pride
That Stripped Away, What Might Have Been Glory

I Should Have Listened To My Heart
And Followed My Inner Voice
But Instead Made A Fool Out Of Me
Now Fear Your Heart I Have Destroyed

Can The Heart Listen To Words Unspoken
Feel The Emotion Left Untouched
I Know What It's Like To Feel The Hurt
When The Spirit Within Me Has Been Crushed

Recalling That Day You Said You Loved Me
But Never Your Actions, Were Spoken
Your Promises I Came To Believe
But From Your Lies, I Had Awoken

I Saw Your Reflection In The Mirror
It Was Not I, That I Saw
But A Part Of Me, I Had To Let Go
And Honey, From You I Had To Withdraw

Why You Could Not See The Truth…
When I Said I Loved You As You Are
Not For Who I Wanted You To Be
That Day We Met, When I Spotted You From Afar

I Blew You A Kiss
You Smiled And Blew One Back
Those Memories Are Now Gone
Erased From My Memory, Absolute Blank

THE UNSEEN THREAD

Beneath The Starlight Of Scattered Stars
In A Constellation So Far Away
When Worlds Collided And New Ones Formed
In A Colossal Explosion Such Majestic Display

They Came A World Apart, Across Different Plains
From A Galaxy, Were Beauty Surrounds
There, A Love Beyond Measures
A Love That Grows Unbound

There, Two Hearts Lost, Wondering
Where The Other One Is
This, The Unwritten Story
One Of Hers, One Of His

To The Heavens, Two Shooting Stars
Clashed, A Shower Of Fragments
Particles Dispersing, Upon This Earth,
Here, The Two Made Their Descent

They Have Never Met
But Perhaps, Through Telepathic Means
Astralling Through The Cosmos
Or Maybe Living In Each Other's Dreams

Two Flames, One Light Shining
Till Their Destiny's End
They Were Connected With
An Unseen Thread

There Lay A Bond Between Them
That Cannot Be Broken
An Invisible Thread Tied Tautly
That Shares A Devotion, A True Love's Token

Soul Mates Till The End
With A Love That's Never Forsaken
Will Never Break Or Fail
One That's Never Forlorn Or Taken

The Unseen Thread, Binding Two Souls
Each With A Woven Story
A Time They Shared With A Glance
They Are Together, Forever Soley

Their Paths Have Converged
A Lasting Instance With A Fleeting Touch
It Is All They Have Needed
Holding Hands Together, Clutched

Pulling Each Other Closer
Two Bodies Wrapped As One
Embracing In The Moment
A Bond, That Cannot Be Undone

The Thread Retains Its Strength
For Together They Have Found Peace
Everlasting Comfort, To Sail
On Their Journey Without Release

A Staring Gaze, Into Each Other's Eyes
The Future Before Them Unfolds
As Their Heartbeats Resounding
With A Vibrance Untold

A Symphony Of Melodies
Beating A Tune Like A Ceremonial Drum
To Last Out Through The Ages and
Neither To Know, What Before Them, Shall Become

This Is A Story Yet To Be Written
Of A Love Connected By An Unseen Thread
That Joins Our Two Soul
And In Time, Will One Day Be Read

As The Music Airs, Bodies Entangling
Dancing, Where Two Become One
Mirroring Each Other's Moves
In A Bond Unbreakable Since They First Begun

Through Distant Spheres They Travelled
When Time And Space Stood Still
An Unseen Thread, That Brought Them Together
Their Destination Now Fulfilled

GRANDMAS KITCHEN

She Lived In A Two Roomed Log Cabin, By The Woods
I'd Visit Her Daily And Watch As She Cooked
A Potbelly Stove In A Corner
Her Utensils, They Were On The Wall, Hooked

That's My Special Grandma, She's Not So Very Old
Took Care Of Me, When I Was Younger
Always Baked Enough For An Army
I Would Never Suffer From Any Hunger

Her Kitchen Was Her Palace
Where She Would Toil And Slave
Kept It Spotless, Days On End
And Her Heart She Always Gave

This Was Grandma's Kitchen, As We Knew It
Everything In Order, Nothing, Out Of Line
That's How I Recall It
As Just A Young Boy Of Nine

Her Hair, Tied In A Tidy Bun
Never, A Strand, Out Of Place
At Times In Her Roller Or Curlers
But Always Worked With Such Grace

In Grandma's Kitchen, With Its Musty Smell
Like Colonial Days Of Times Long Ago
Wooden Tables And Chairs
This I Imagined, I Did Not Know

The Smell Of Her Cooking, Pleasantly Lingered
Wearing Her Apron, In A Floral Display
She Knew What To Cook The Family
Shelling Beans For Supper That Day

I Was Young And Small Growing Up
Standing On A Bucket To Reach The Sink
I Helped To Peel The Potatoes
She'd Smile And Send Me A Wink

Sundays, At Grandma's Kitchen, I Looked Forward,
Her Baking Cakes And Biscuits Were Her Best
Roast Dinner In The Oven, Below The Stained Stove
Always An Occasion, When I Was Nicely Dressed

Dinner Was Served With The Finest Cutlery
On A Table Built For Four, With Candle Light
A Feast, Fit For Kings
We Were Poor, But Had Enough, Despite

That Evening, Sang Songs With Laughter And Joy
Gas Heater To Shake The Cold Away
Cocoa, We Drank And Roasted Marshmallows
Was Hoping, That Day Would Stay

Remembering Those Times Fondly
In My Grandma's Kitchen
Was Always Homely To Family And Friends
She Worked Hard, No Fuss Or Bitchin

They Were The Everlasting Memories To Treasure
When I Feel Lonely, I'll Think Of Her
In My Grandma's Kitchen
Remembering How We Were

IS-SALEB TA MALTIN
(Maltese Cross)

A Symbol Of Protection
A Badge Of Honour For Which We Wear
An Eight-Pointed Cross, Is-Saleb Ta Maltin
Only The Brave Got To Bear

From The Crusaders, The Knights Of St John
Who Laid Their Lives For Fellow Man
Through Kindness And Devotion
Back When Malta Siege Began

These Gallant Maltese Crusades
Wore Is-Saleb Tal Maltin
An Emblem For Their Heroic Deeds
Protected The Island They Fought In

Is-Saleb Tal Maltin Awarded
To A Small Southern Mediterranean Isle
That Fought In Wars And Bravely Won
With Pride And A Noble Style

Is-Saleb Ta Maltin
Gained For Devotion And Patriotic Valour
By The Sovereign Military Order
When Enemies Landed On Maltese Shores

Is Saleb Tal Maltin
Adorned On Every Heraldic Crest
A Nation's Glory,
Triumphant In Their Quest

Is Salib Tal Maltin
Revered And Cherished
An Identity That Sets Us Apart
To Remember Who Before Us Have Perished

BETRAYAL

We Shared A Bond That

Could Never Be

Broken

You Took My Hands

Promised To Love Me

Forever

When We Married For

Better, For Worse, Those

Words We Had

Spoken

Cheat On Me, You

Said You Would

Never

You Hid Behind The Truth

With Lies, And Utter

Betrayal

I Was Never Good Enough,

So, You Sought Else

Where

The Mother Of Your Children

But In Return, You Lived In

Denial

Our Love You Broke, The

Trust You Shattered. This

Life I Couldn't

Bear

Betrayal, Devoid Of All Romance
Love So Scarce, Only
The Lingering
Memories.
My Heart, Scarred, Lashed
And Beaten, By Words You Had
Said
Your Raged Bitter Anger
Behind Closed Doors, No One Ever
Sees
Shattered Hope, Shattered Dreams
Betrayal, By Rumours You
Spread
"I Love You" Just Words
Floating In The
Air
With Empty Meaning,
Your Love That Cannot Be
Reclaimed
Told Me Once, You'd Never Hurt
And Love Me Forever, Said
Your Life You'd
Share
All That Remains, A Candle
With Its Burnt Out
Flame

TULIPS

From Bulbs They Quickly Grew
Stems, Standing Firm Against The Wind
Two By Two Planted In The Orchard Rows
And Too, Nearby Pastures, Filled

Parading Before Him, In Fields Of Gold
Tulips, In A Symphony Of Colours
They Sway Into The Breeze
Waiting To Be Picked By Lovers

An Artist, His Easel At Hand
A Palette Of Colours Array
His Blank Canvas Comes To Life
In Full Glory, These Tulips Display

Colours Bursting, As They Bloom
With Every Stroke He Makes
To Capture This Timeless Beauty
Carefully, So Details Ought Not Escape

In These Fleeting Moments
He Knows they Will Not Last Forever
Frantically Paint Splatters
To Capture Before Him, This Treasure

These Tulips, Side By Side
Adorning The Country View
In The Zephr Breeze, They Gently Sway
Many More, Purple, Reds The Pink And Blue

That Reflect The Sun
Their Fragrance In The Wind Journeys
With Petals Light And Soft
Nothing As Grandeur Such As These

I Picked From That Field
For My Lady Mine
A Tulip, Petals Of Scarlet Amber
That Nature Had Defined

Nature's Canvas So Pure And Bright
Tulips, Grazing Undisturbed
When Spring Be Nigh Upon Us
Then Their Grace, We Will Have Earned

And While Nature, Upon Them Kiss
These Long-Stemmed Timeless Beauties
Appeared To Have Winked At Me
No Such Sight, As Beautiful As These

Filled With A Passion
To Give To Your True Love
A Token Of Affection
And Tell Them What You're Thinking Of

Tulips, That Bless Us With Their Charm
To Show The Beauty In All We Possess
And Admire The Life We Hold
To Accept Nothing Less

MAMA TOLD ME

She's Not Here To Share With Me
The Fruits Of Her Wisdom
But Growing Up, I Began To Realise
A Mother's Love Is Never Done

Mama Told Me, Baby! You Gonna Be Somebody
Don't Be Afraid, With Your Head Held High
Be That Person You Wanted To Be
Give Yourself A Chance, Gotta Give It A Try

Many Times I'd Fallen, "Get Up, She Would Say"
You Can Succeed, If You Only Allow
These Words, Just Echo Within Me
Thinking About Her, I Realise It Now

Mama Told Me, Love Yourself Before Another
Coz Maybe Alone You Will Be One Day
To Love The Woman, You Will Become
Accept Yourself First Before Others May

I Remember Her Words Of Guidance Well
I Was In My Teens, Learning About Life
"I Will Have Your Back", She Would Often Say
When I Needed Help, Making Someone A Good Wife

Mama Told Me Respect Yourself As In Others
Never Take Things For Granted
Sometimes Miracles Do Come True
And Life, On A Silver Platter, Is Never Handed

"You Won't Know Everything Child,"
So Be Willing To Grow, To Learn
That Day Will Come, When Good Things Will
Come And Respect You Will Also Earn

I've Learnt To Live Without, When Money Ran Scarce
"It Won't Buy You Happiness", This So Often Said
Rely Upon Yourself, The Best You Can
You Will Be Showered A Greater Love Instead

I Have Learnt A Lot, In What Mama Told Me
That Beyond Every Dark Cloud High Above
There Is The Sun With A Glimmer Of Hope
And A Joy When You Find Your Secret Love

I Have Found Guidance In What Mama Told Me
The Good Advice, For Ever I'll Cherish
She's Not Here To Share My Joys And Sadness
Will Treasure Her Always, Till The Day I Perish

SOMETHING INSIDE

Something Inside, I

Couldn't Let

Go

These Where The Memories

I Kept For So

Long

We Made Moments That

Would Last

Forever

But The Day You Sailed Away,

Reasons, I Did Not

Know

Doubts Filled My Mind,

If I Really, With Him I

Belonged

Always Kept Him In Thought

And Forgetting, I'd

Never

Something Inside Said "Let Go"

How Can I, He's Always On My

Mind

When I Fall Asleep, I've No

Where To

Escape

The Dreams That Follow, Haunt

My Living

Life

And Even Here, Peace I

Cannot Yet

Find

Vision Of Betrayal, Slowly

Begin To Take

Shape

Talking Behind My Back, Like

Stabbing With A Jagged Edged

Knife

Something Inside, A Voice

"Stay And Fight"

Your Hearts Will Stand

United

"Don't Let Pride, Stand

In Your

Way

When The Walls That Were

Built, Will Sooner Crumble, Then

Part

Then Your Mind Be Set Free

And Body To Body

Undivided

There With Each Other,
Till You're Old And
Grey
My Thoughts Of Being Alone
I Could Not Bear To Be
Apart
I Fell To My Knees And Prayed
He Would
Return
While Something Inside,
The Urge To Get Back Up, To
Arise
Though The Many Times
I Had
Fallen
I Had To Believe, He Will Be
Faithful, And My Love He Must
Earn
But So Hard To Consider, So Hard
To Trust, With All His Savage
Lies
I Knew At That Moment
There Was Something
Inside

FOLLOW YOUR DREAM

It's A Big World Out There Son
You Can Be Anything You Put Your Mind On
A School Teacher, An Astronaut
And If You're Smart Enough, A Surgeon

Whatever Your Heart Desires
I Will Be Besides You Every Step Of The Way
So Much That You Can Achieve
But Be The Best, No Matter, What One May Say

"If You Fall, Find The Courage To Get Back Up"
Search For The Strength From Within
Opportunities Are At Your Fingertips
And Never Lose Sight Of Your Vision

Listen To That Voice Inside
The Voice, Telling You, Not To Ever Quit
Stand Tall, Stand Proud, And
Never, To You Failures, Admit

Before Success, My Son
There Will Be Failure Many Times
Don't Hold Back, Following Your Dreams
Always Before You. Many Mountains To Climb

Son! I Can See Your Ambitious Passion
When I Look In Your Eyes, Filled With A Burning Desire
A Yearning For Inner Growth
I Feel Will Take You Higher

Don't worry about the price tag
How much you will make
And don't run away, if you feel your
World is ending, but learn from the mistakes

Follow Your Dream, Wherever It May Lead
Don't Live For Someone Else's
It Is Your Dream To Follow
It's Your Choice, To Choose How To Express It

Son! I Know You Are Only Just Ten
I'll Not Always Be Around To Tell You
To Guide, In What You Will Accomplish, But,
I Know You Will Find Greatness, In All That You'll Do

Someday You Will Have Children
And Teach To Follow Their Dreams
To Never Lose Hope, Or Heart, To Strive
No Matter How Difficult Problems Seem

Nothing "Succeeds Like Success" Son
You Must Have A Vision, A Plan
However Big, However Small
And I Trust In You, To Do All You Can

WHEN DESTINY CALLS

From The Time We Are

Born, Till The Time Of Our

Demise

Like A Road Map With

Endless Routes And Tangled

Highways

We'll Search For That Coveted

Truth, Looking Yonder
Above Us -Blue
Skies

When Destiny Calls, A Future

Not Yet Planned, A Guiding

Touch Shall Lead The

Ways

We Can Write Our Own Destiny
For Our Future's Not Yet
Set

Our Dreams Will Inspire

As We Journey On A Life Long

Plan

Opportunities Knocking, Take In

Both Hands, Moments To

Savour No Sorrows No

Regrets

Head Held High, You're
Gonna Make It, Make It
This I Know You
Can

Too Afraid To Face What's
Ahead, Afraid To Delve Into Another
Plan
When Destiny Calls, Will
Your Heart, In It
Embrace
To Show The World, The
Person Within You, And
Be That Better
Man
To Have The Courage
And Face Your Demons
May You Never Fall From
Grace
When Destiny Calls, Will
You Rise Above Your Fears, And
Knock Down
Obstacles
Those Hurdles Of Life At
Times Have Set You
Back
Many Times, You Tried
Many Times, You Failed,
But
Triumphed, When Thought
Impossible

WHAT SHE WANTED, WASN'T WORDS

We Spoke From Worlds Apart
Only That I Knew She Was Unique
Wasn't Sure Exactly How Or Why
But I Knew, With Her, I Had To Speak

Shyly I'd Ask For Her Photo
Sure, Hesitant To Mention
But Took This As An Adventure
Had To Grab At Her Attention

Was I Was Too Forward
So Desperate To Try
Nothing Ventured, Nothing Gained
I Keep Asking Myself Why

As Her Smiles Gleamed Upon My Sight
So Did The Inspiration's Glow
Laying There Besides Me
My Creative Juices Flowed

Her Presence Ignited My Every Thought
Putting Pen To Paper, I Started To Begin
I Noted Every Word, But Wasn't My
Writing She Was Interested In

We Chuckled, As I Knew
What She Wanted, And It Wasn't Words
A Sensitive Touch, A Warm Embrace
To Feel Her Contoured Curves

My Eyes Lit Up,
To Her Shapely Gentle Bends
Body Trembling, Tightly Fisted
Excitement, To My Body Did Send

She Was My Motivation
My Guidance, My Light
When Words Couldn't Capture,
Hope Gave Me Reasons To Write

We Made Plans To One Day Meet
And Years Upon Years We Finally Met
Flashbacks Came Flooding, How
She Was That Beauty, I Did Not Forget

Hi! How Are You?
She Greeted Me With Warmth
Arms Around Me, With A Comforting Hug
Meeting, At The Hub Of The North

Wasting No Time, I Took Her Hand
Drenched In A Nervous Sweat
From The Jitters As Our Eyes Met
Something, I'll Never Forget

Eyes Don't Lie, Told Myself
What She Wanted, Wasn't Words
We've Only Just Spoken After All
And Came From Different Worlds

Into Her Car, We Drove Away
A Bite To Eat, Was A Nice Thought
Right About Now, To McDonalds
And Shouted Her A Meal, As I Had Ought

Played "Footsies" Under The Table
Like Children We Seemed
I Knew I Get A Reaction
Well! At Least She Never Screamed

What She Wanted Wasn't Words
I Knew What She Had In Mind
Her Hands Drew Closer To Mine
That Night, Pleasing A Man, Like She Was Designed

Breakfast In Bed, The Order Of The Day
Belly Full, And A Smile Upon Her Face
Couldn't Be More Happier
I Knew I Was In The Right Place

It Was A Memorable Time,
Those Short Moments, I Tell You Truly
What Was Her Name Again?
Janet, Ginnette Or Julie

Today My Thoughts Escapes Me
But Oh! How I Fondly Wish To Remember
Just That Hourglass Of Time Ticks On
It Was, I Recall One Late September

How Funny It Was To Recall
That Was She Wanted, Wasn't Words
I Can Laugh About It Now
And One Day Soon, My Memory Will Serve

PAY IT FORWARD

One Good Random Act Of Compassion
Deserves Another,
A Smile To A Stranger,
Your Neighbour, Your Brother

To Treat Someone Kindly, No Rewards Expected
May Change A Life, Or Give One
Pay It Forward, To Those Who Have Little
Their Respect, You May Have Already Won

Pay It Forward, Let Someone Know You Care
Expect From Them, Nothing In Return
Their Smiles Will Speak For Themselves
And From Their Lives, You'll Do Well To Learn

It Only Takes A Moment Of Your Time
To Give Service To Those Heavy Laden
In Return, Wealth, Not Of Earthly Riches
Will Come Your Way, This I Know Be Certain

When You Pay It Forward And Pass It On
The World, Be A Better Place
The Concept, Is Really Nothing New
Around For Generations, What Makes This Human Race

Pay It Forward, Do Someone A Favour
Forgiving Their Mistakes,
They Will Forgive Yours, In Return
A Little Love, A Little Trust, Is All It Takes

As The World Turns With Selfishness
Lend A Hand To Those In Need
It Helps Brighten Up Their Day, And
Like The Growth Of A Flower, Starts Of From A Seed

To Change Our Ways, Starts From A Single Notion
Like A Seedling, Rising To A Giant Oak
Its Branches Reaching For The Light
Just As That Seedling, Your Love Cannot Be Cloaked

Pay It Forward And Help Carry A Load
A Friendly Shoulder, Or A Word Just To Say Hello
No Need For A Reason To Spread The Kindness
And Just Like That Oak, Love Will Grow

In The End, Peace Will Find Its Way To Your Heart
Where Compassion Dwells And Love Takes Hold
Pay It Forward, With No Strings Attached
Look All Around, Then Watch, What Will Unfold

Their Lives Which You've Changed,
And In Turn, They Too Paid Forward With Deeds,
Of Goodness And Giving Back
When Others Were In Their Times Of Needs

SOMETIMES ITS HARD

Go To Your Room, I Heard Him Say
I Knew That Moment, Wasn't Looking Good
That Look, I've Seen Before, Mama Just Watched
He Sat Down Beside Me, Said If I Understood

He Raised A Hand, I Almost Cried
With That Gesture, Just Patted My Head
"I Brought You This For Your Birthday"
"I Hope You Like It", My Heart Raced, Just Sped

Happy Tears Ran Down My Cheek
"I Haven't Been Much Of A Father, Son"
But Hope We Can Start Again, Be Friends
I Only Wish I Can Take Back, The Bad, I've Done

With Excitement, I Open The Wrappings
Much As I've Always Wanted, A Train Set
He Looked At Me, With A Smile
I Was Only Seven, Something I Wouldn't Forget

He Walked Out Of The Room, Gave Mum A Hug
I Knew, That Moment, Things Would Change
"Im Sorry, How I've Treat You, Over Years
I Want To Make It Up, Our Vows, We Should Exchange

Sometimes Its Hard, Looking Back Now
We Hurt The Ones Who Are Dear
His Words Are Forgotten, But The Marks Remain
Seems Like Yesterday, But Ever So Clear

I Grew Up Learning, Abuse Wasn't Right
Leaves The Body In Psychological Bruises
And A Life In Disarray, What Is Real, What Is Not
One Can Elect The Right, If So Chooses

Sometimes It Is Hard, No One To Trust
A Mother Or A Father, Someone You Admire
Can Leave You In Doubt Or Question,
What Beliefs That Will Transpire

I Was Young Then, And Didn't Know Better
Did What I Was Told, And Listened
But Understand Now, He Had A Drinking Problem
And From This Family Kept His Distance

LOOK INSIDE

I Am A Man Without A Home

No Place To Reside, No One To Call My

Own

I Am Just Like You, Breathe The Same Air

I Speak With The Same

Words

But You Look At Me And

Just Tend To Walk

Away

The Sidewalks, The Parks

Is All The Shelter Ive

Known

No Family Do I Possess

Im One With The Trees And The

Birds

My Heart, Too Does Feel,

Look Inside, And Hope Awhile You Will

Stay

People Amble By The Busy Streets

No Notice They Take To Wonder Who I

Am

I Am Nobody Special

Just A Man, Without A

Home

I Have No Luxury, A Bed, A Tv,
Just A Cardboard
Crate
Do You Really Wonder Of My Life
To Care Or Give A
Damn
Where I Go Or Sleep At Night
When Deserted Streets I
Roam
Will You Wonder Of My Next Meal
Or Will Nothing Fill Up My
Plate
Ill Be Fighting With Scavenging Rats,
The Water, From A Drain
Pipe
Any Scraps Will Do, Driven By Hunger
A Morsel Or A Bite Will
Do
Look Inside Me, My Life's Not
Five Star
Hotel
Clothes, In Tatters, My Face In Grime
Scarcely A Shower, No Towel To
Wipe

No Moments Of Pleasure,
Cept, Moths Circling Street Lamps Of
Neon Rays In Yellows, And Green
Hues
Around The Corner, Waste And Debris
To Add, To The Putrid
Smell
The Nights Are Lonely And Long
Will The Day, Ever
Break
No Concept Of Time, As I Awaken To The
Freshness Of The
Breeze
Upon My Face That Caresses
The Contours, With
Grace
In Coldness, Fingers Numb
Gotta Get Up, This Journey, Must Continue To
Make
Weather Five Below, "Move Your Body"
Stay Warm, Before It Will
Freeze"
Deep In Thoughts, Salvation,
Anybody, With Whom I Can
Embrace

Or Die Here With Nothing But My Name
Who, Today Will Really
Care
Has Humanity Abandoned Me
And Left Me
Betrayed
Will I Die, And Buried Without
A Reasonable
Cause
Look Inside Me, And Walk
In My Shoes, If You Really
Dare
And If You Meet Me, Don't Walk Away
I Beg, Don't Be
Afraid
And When You Walk Away
Back To The Highlife And Family
Please Remember As I
Was

X'HEMM MOHBI - (What Is Hidden)

X'hemm Mohbi, Beneath The Surface
Under The Deceit, The Rumours You Spread
I Tried To Believe You
But Couldn't Fathom What You Had Said

What Fibs, Concealed, When You Said What You Did?
Saying You Loved Me, And To Be With Me
Or Was It A Mask You Used, To Conceal
The Shaded Truth, To Set Me Free

Maybe You Really Didn't Care, You
Left Me In Pieces, A Million Fragments, Shattered
I Guess I Wasn't Important Enough
Not That You Cared, Or That I Even Mattered

X'hemm Mohbi, Around Your Smile,
Buried Within You, Deep Way Inside
I Know That You're Laughing At Me Now
What Is It Really, That You Want To Hide

Is It The Truth You Are Trying To Dodge?
When You Stand Before Me, And Pretend You Cared
I Don't Need Your Pity, So Please Just Go
And Take With You, The Love We Once Shared

Whatever Dwells Unseen, Deep In Your Callous Heart
Will Never Be Freed. There To Always Remain
The Lies, There Etched Shan't Ever Escape
To Hurt, Or Will No Longer Cause Me Pain

X'hemm Mohbi, That There Are Things I Cannot See
They Lie Buried, Hidden Beneath
Disguised, Like The Truth, You Imagine Is Real
Let Me Go, Just Let Me Breathe,

To Carry On This Life, Without You In It
Take The Love You Pretended Was Real, But Fake
In A Life You Lived, Like A Masquerade
You Took Everything, What Is Left To Take?

X'hemm Mohbi, When You Stand Before Me
In Your Cast Silhouette Outline?
Your Well-Kept Secrets And Your stories
To This Day Still Hide Behind

WALKING ON EGGSHELLS

The Silence In The Air As He Walks On By
Being Careful Not To Walk On Eggshells
She's Living In Fear Inside Her Head
The Constant Worry As If In A Prison Cell

Caution, Take Heed, She Will Hear
Every Word That Passes Your Lips
Every Move, Every Step
From Her Mind, Her Sanity Strips

Thread Lightly When Passing
Care Not To Interrupt Her Solitude
Ears Will Be Listening, Eyes, Watching
Her Heightened Perceptions, Attuned

Walking On Eggshells
Fragmented Pieces Chipping Away
Tranquillity Filled The Room
In Here, hesitating to Stay

Did I Say Something Wrong,
Seeing It Upon Her Face
The Feeling Of Blame Fell Upon Me
And Her Trust, I Could Not Replace

Giving Me A Discomforting Look
Placing Her Hand Upon My Shoulder
As A Teardrop Fell From Her Eyes
As I Moved Forward To Approach Her

Her Spirit Appeared Broken
Emotions, Betrayed, Desolate
She's Been Hurt, Hurt Before
By Nothing, To Which She Will Admit

I Knew Something Mattered
She Would Not Say
"It's Ok, You Can Tell Me"
But Motioned, To Go Away

Was Like Walking On A Tightrope
One Slip, Could Be Your Last
Every Action, Every Notion
Could Rekindle Her Troubled Past

She Is Fragile, A Body Feeble And Broken
Trust Has Deserted Her, Now Just A Word
Doesn't Use Or Even Utter
In Fact, Just Been Never Heard

I Realised In That Moment
That Something Was Wrong…
When Walking On Eggshells, A Sense
Of Insecurity, Feeling You Don't Belong

She Speaks To No-One
Been Hurt Many Times Before
A Forsaken Past, There, Does Not Dwell
Choosing To Close Its Door

Her Secrets, Tactfully Well Kept
In A Portion Of Her Mind, Hidden
Silence Upon Us Falls
And Only The Fear Of Hate, In Her's Ridden

I Daren't Speak Of What Has Gone Before
As Memories, Become Now Obscured
You Can Hear A Pin Drop In The Stillness Of The Room
From The Recollection, Of The Yesterdays She Endured

She's A Sole Maiden, Never Married
Living Alone In A Cottage Home
Cept' A Cat Keeping Her Company
Only Trust, She's Ever Known

People Just Pass On By
Caring Not To Walk On Eggshells
A Whisper Can Travel Afar
As She Knows So Very Well

They Daren't Upset Her Turf
Just Don't Come Too Near
With Tears That Fall From Her Eyes
These, The Tears Of Loneliness, You'll Hear

There Was Something Ominous
About The Way She Appeared
I Felt Something Was Up, But Wouldn't Say
Her Health Was In Danger I Feared

Nothing Could Have Prepared Me
For What Was About To Come
Taking A Knife Into Her Hand
Not Knowing, Where This Had Stemmed From

Putting It To Her Wrist
Yes, It Was Just A Butter Knife
With No Intent To Use
Perhaps To Take Her Own Life

"You're Scaring Me Now Dear
I Wish You Wouldn't"
Putting It Away, As She Laughed It Off
She'd Have Done It, Had I Not Been Present

Today, As You Pass By Her Cottage
A "Do Not Disturb Sign" Hangs Upon Her Door
Peering Through The Kitchen Windows
No Signs Of Life, Just Lying On The Floor

Is She Even Alive?
As Mail, Gathered Outside On The Step
A Notebook That Laid Besides Her
With The Word That Read "Help"

LET ME DOWN SOFTLY

When You Walk Out The Door
Because We Had A Lovers Spat
Please Let Me Down Softly
Losing You, My Heart Cannot Take That

I Know I Did You Wrong
But Tried To Make Amends
It Was Always Your Side Of The Story
Saying You Loved Me, You Only Would Pretend

My World Was Built Around You
In Everything That I Did Or Say
The Flowers On Valentines
And Presents On Every Special Day

Let Me Down Softly, When
You Say, You're Never To Return
And Like A Puppet, Pulling My Strings
Controlling, Till I Crashed And Burned

You're Always Too Busy
To Busy To Call Me On The Phone
Did You Ever Think I May Be Missing You
Or That You're The First I've Ever Known

No, I'm Not Crying For Redemption
I'm Not Looking For Sympathy
You Won't Have Me Fooled
Into Thinking I'm Some Love Sick Puppy

If You Wanna Be Leaving, Then Go
But When You Walk Out That Door
Don't Look Back, I Won't Be There
Your Love To Me, I Cannot Restore

When You Hugged Me,
Felt Like A Chilled Embrace
I Felt Your Love, Slipping Away Escape
I Know, One Day, It Is That, I Will Replace

I Know Ahead, There's No Beacon Of Light
To Save Us Now
All Inside Me, Now Is Darkness
And Still I Cannot Understand How

Let Me Down Softly
When You Look Into My Eyes
And A Lonely Tear Runs Down My Cheek
But, I Know, In Time, My Spirit Will Rise

To Be A Better Man, Stronger
I Have Learnt My Fate
Accepting The Inevitable
I Don't Dislike You, Or Even Hate

Could You Find A Way To Release Me
From Your Clutches
And Spare Me The Grief
Of Whatever It Touches

I Won't Beg You To Say, If You Turned
And Walked Out From All That Is Me
But Please Let Me Down Softly
And Like A Bird, Set Me Free

Was There Ever Place In Your Universe
Some Place I Could Revolve Around
You'd Be The Queen, And I, The Pillar
Your Strength Unbound

Before You Let Me Down Softly
Give Me A Little More Time
To Show How Much I Care
I Know, Together, Our Love Shall Climb

But I Cannot Do It, Feeling So Lost
With The Hurt, Stuck Deep Inside
Etched Within Me, Embedded
I've Tried, God Only Knows, I've Tried

Whatever It Takes, But Please Let Me Try
You're The Missing Piece
I Cannot Do Without
To Soothe My Inner Peace

GIVE ME A SECOND CHANCE

I Know I Have Messed Up

And Let You

Down

But Give Me A Second Chance

To Show You My

Worth

I Promise To Never Fool

Around, Or Play A Circus

Clown

I'll Be There Always To Shower

You With Love, Side By Side, On This

Earth

Let Me Turn Your Frowns Into Smiles

Your Nights Into

Day

Where There Be Sadness

Let Me Be Your

Joy

Give Me Another Chance,

I Beg, Never Turn Me

Away

To Be With You, Today And

Always, Together In This Life To

Enjoy

I Know Mistakes, In My

Life I Have

Made

I've Realised I Have Hurt You

Not Meaning To, Or Knowing

How

But Losing Your Affection, Unconditional

Love, Was The Price I

Paid

I Hope There Can Be An Us

As Once There Was, If Only You'd

Allow

No Tears Have I Left To Shed

No More Joy Left To

Share

Give Me A Second Chance

To Prove Myself Of

Value

Let You Be The One To

Whom I Would Greatly

Care

Be One With Me Jointly,

To See What We Can

Do

Give Me A Second Chance
For Our Future's Same Path,
Road
Where We Can Walk Hand In Hand
Perhaps Down The Wedded
Aisle
Where Our Vows We'll Share
And Love, To Our Friends, We've
Showed
Let Me Remember That Day
For A Moment In Time, Or Perhaps
Awhile

SEASONS OF MY LIFE

How Could I Forget You, When You Came Into My Life?
You Taught Me That Life's Worth Living
Taught Me Courage To Be Strong
To Understand, My Love, Deserved To Be Given

In The Seasons Of My Life,
You Were There To Make Things Right
Gave Me Hope When I Despaired
Turned My Darkness Into Light

Never Did I Doubt, It Was You I Came To Seek
Came Out Of My Dreams, To Stand Before Me
Your Smiles Pierced Through My Heart
Wondered Really, If You Could Really Be…

That Person, To Share The Seasons Of My Life
Be In The Harshest Winds Or Winter Chills
To Pick Me Up Like The Autumn Leaves
Or Rescue Me From The Ails And Ills

You Are The Reasons That I Live
In The Seasons Of My Life,
Like Nature, When Seeds Are Planted
They Thrive Through Cold And Bitter Strife

Somewhere, There's A Place In The Fields Of Gold
Where Brightly Flowers Bloom
Petals Of Yellow, Take To The Breeze
Taking With Them Their Scented Perfume

These Fragrant Flowers That I Pick
To Bring Me Closer, With You, I'll Share
To Show My Unwavered Devotion
To Show, How Much I Truly Care

The Seasons Of My Life Began With You
When You Picked Me Up, Falling To The Ground
You Nursed Me To Health
No Other Like You, Honey, I Have Found

Maybe It Was Love At First Sight
I'm Truly Sorry, If I Seem, To Really Not Know
By Some Cosmic Attraction To You, Drawn
And It Was Your Heart, You Came To Show

There Is No Other Person, Dearest As You
Who Have Comforted Me, during The Seasons
Of My Life, That Has Come To Be,
No Explanations Needed, Just No Other Reasons

MY DUSTBIN DREAMS

A Solitary Cardboard Box, My Home
That's Nestled Upon This Curb
This Is My Mansion, When I Have Not A Home
A Place Where No One Needs Disturb

I Hear Them Whisper "What A Bum
Go Get A Job"
Little Do They Understand
That My Life Was Robbed

My Possessions, Taken
Family That I Once Knew, Left Me Abandoned
Had A High Paying Job
Got Sick, Now On The Streets, Stranded

It Is This Curb, That I've
Come To Embrace
A Loner, No Friends, I Can Call Mine
And Here, I Can Call My Place

May Not Seems Like Much I Know
But What I Have, Can Call Mine
In My Dustbin Dreams
Where I Can Dream Of A Casket Of Wine

With Family And Friends
Around The Table Laughing, Singing
Talking About Family
How It Was In The Beginning

Besides Me, A Street Lamp
That's My Only Light
At Times Does Flicker
In The Solitude Of The Night

Cold And Chilly Cobbled Stones
That Catch The Wintery Chills
Whilst The City Sleeps Snuggly Tight
I Fight To Stay Alive, As The Snow, Around Me Spills

Rugged Up In A Shabby Blanket
Patched Up From All The Holes
No Matches, For A Fire To Light
To Save This Old Soul

Numb Fingers, Dressed In Mittens
To Steer The Cold Away
As My Breath Crystallizes
On This Wintery Day

All My Possession, And These Are Few
Stored Neatly, Neatly In My Dustbin
What Matters To Me
I Keep Tucked Within

A Cardboard House, Neath The
Clouds Of Mist And Haze
Snow Flakes Drizzling, Piled At My Feet
It Will Be, For Many More Days

This Life, So Battered, Bruised And Worn
Hopeful, In What Lies Ahead In My Dustbin's Dreams
For I Know There Will Be Treasures
In Spite Of What Lies Ahead In Life's Schemes

In These Dustbin's Dreams
Where Shadows Lie
I Will Always Be, Society's Outcast
Who Will Never See Eye To Eye

There Is No Self Worth
This I Have Come To Believe
Thrown Away, Rejected, A Cast Out
With Nothing More To Achieve

Fighting For Life, Against Alley Cats
For Scraps, Just To Survive
Rats In A Distance, Spying What Little I've Got
Awaiting A Meal, For When It Arrives

It's Just Another Day, Another Fight
Kill Or Be Killed, The Saying Goes
For Scraps And Morsels
And Whatever Life Throws

This Crusty Bread, Oh! What A Treat
Perhaps A Slice Of Bacon, An Egg Or Two
Now I Am Dreaming
Ok, How About A Carafe Of Red, Too

My Stories To Tell, Of My Life's That Been,
A Discarded Remnants Of Humanity
Where No One Needs To Know Me
As Far That I Could See

For I Know, Little Do They Care
Or Where I've Been Or Going
I Want To Find A Way To Rise Above
Perhaps A Home With A Love That's Growing

My Dustbin Dreams Is All That I Possess
What Others Consider Garbage
I Find The Beauty That Lies Within
And Within It, There Is Something Big

Every Night, I Rummage Through
For Perhaps A Surprise, But Alas Not
The Usual Tatters Is What I Find And
A Dingy Loaf, That I Did Spot

A Chipped Old Plate
And A Chocolate Bar For Two
They Mayn't Seem Like Much
I'd Have Felt Blessed, Had They Been New

My Plastic Knife And Fork, Ain't No
Silverware Or Fitting For A King
But My Home Is This Cardboard Mansion
My Kingdom, That Means Just Everything

I'm Still Alive Amidst Life's Chaos
No Warmth To Comfort Me
But Oh! What A Life, Free To Come And Go
Do As I Wish, I Am, From Society. Free

THE FURY OF THE SEA

Darkness Swept Across The Sea
Clouds Of Grey Summoned The Storm
There, To Ignite With A Thunderous Roar
Like An Orchestral Band Waiting To Perform

As Lightening Zaps Over The Sky
The Thunder Echoed With A Mighty Clap
Fiercely It Fought In Nature's Rage
Bombarded The Scene, With A Violent Snap

The Fury Of The Sea
With Its Swirling Tides
Awakens, When Savage Winds Howled
Disturbing The Tranquillity As Oceans Collide

While Waves Clashed, Like Titans Battle
They Leapt And Would Sway,
As Nature Rages Without Warning
Shooting Out Its Misty Spray

Deep In The Distant Horizon
Ships Like Children's Toys, Jostled
Like Paper Boats, Tossed
Up Into The Air, Hurled

The Sounds Of Sirens,
If You Listen Carefully, Can Be Heard
Seducing With Their Alluring Voices
Young Sailors Their Minds They Stirred

And Sent Them To Their Doom
On One Ill-Fated Journey
When The Skyscape Opened Up
They Were, At God's Holy Mercy

As The Rains From The Heavens Open Up
A Mighty Force, Rumbles Across The Land
When The Wild Seas Embrace
No Structure, Could Ever Withstand

With A Forty Foot Raging Swell,
Ships Are Bombarded In The Duel Of Waves
Against The Height, Of An Oceanic Wall
That Sent Sailors To Their Watery Graves

In The Fury Of The Seas
Foaming Giant Waves Crashed Upon The Shore
Untamed And Uncontrolled
That One, Could Not Ignore

When The Morning Came
Silence Fell Upon The Shoreline
The Force Of Nature Slowly Calmed
And The Sounds Of Fury, Had Declined

Blue Skies, The Following Morn
What Was Once So Savage And Fierce
Now Birds In Flocks Across The Distance
Squawking With A Shrill That Pierced

In The Fury Of The Sea
We Saw The Beauty Of It All
Though Seemingly Untamed
It Answered To Nature's Call

WALK IN MY SHOES

The Burdens I Have Suffered,
And The Joys I Have Seen
You Cannot Know, Till You've Walked In My Shoes
To The Places I Have Been

You Say You Know Me, But Do You Really
My Thoughts Are My Own, Delicately Hidden
You Look At Me Quizzically
As If To Understand What's In My Mind, Written

Don't Say You Know How I Feel
Or That You Feel My Hurt
Feel My Wounds, See Into My Past
And Learn, That I Too Have Been Burnt

Walk In My Shoes, Take A Load
Of My Shoulders, Heavy Laden
Does Your Heart Ache When You Cannot Carry
Much Further And Your Spirit… Broken

Have You Ever Walked In My Shoes
To Say "No" To Your Baby And Couldn't Choose
Because You Can't Afford To Buy Milk
Or Replace Her Worn-Out Shoes

Try To Walk In My Shoes
When You Cannot Enjoy Mere Luxuries
Of Life, The Essential Things
Like The Weekly Groceries

The Simple Things Of Life
A Walk In The Park, A Swim In The Sea
Because You're Wheelchair Bound
Or Watch A Movie, Coz You Cannot See

To Listen To The Sound Of Chirping Birds
Because You've Gone Deaf
Yes, Those Simple Pleasures Of Life
And Losing Faith, Within Yourself

We'll Take For Granted,
What We Have Always Known
Those, Perhaps The Necessities Of Life
I Pray, You'll Never Feel Alone

Walk In My Shoes, Tell Me What It's Like
I Am Happy Just To Get By
Happy When You Don't Discriminate
We Can Be Friends, If You Only Try…

I Am A Person Much The Same
That Feels The Happy, Sad Emotions
Seeing You Laugh At My Worn-Out Clothes
Just Sorry, I Don't Have The Same Things

You Jeer At Me, As You Walk Passed
"Get A Job, You Lazy Bum"
Walk In My Shoes, Not Knowing
When Your Next Meal Will Come

Or If You Fall Ill, Without Medications
Because You Couldn't Afford
Walk In My Shoes, Over Countless Miles
Then You Cry, When You Life Has Been Ignored

I'm Not Looking For Sympathy
Just Understanding, To Be Aware
Don't Feel Pity,
Because I Know You Really Don't Care

Walk In My Footsteps, Care Not To Stumble
For There Are Numerous Potholes
Of Life, Believe Me, There Are A Lot
Losing Your Friends… Many, Such As Those

When You Walk In My Shoes
Are You Not Afraid, Not Waking
The Following Day, To Inhale Another Breath
Or If Another Mouthful. You'll Be Taking

Walk In My Shoes And Feel The Fears
When Every Day, Could Be You Last
Bills Not Paid Or Hungry Mouths Unfed
Would Anyone Really Know, If Never Asked

Though They See You Scrounging Around
For A Morsel To Eat
From Every Bin, At Every Park
Then Sleeping The Night In A Park Bench Seat

Not A Dime To Your Name,
No Family To Entrust Upon
You Only To Rely Upon Yourself
What Else Have You To Go On

Walk In My Shoes, To Know What I Go Through
Not Knowing What I Have Seen
The Hurdles I've Had To Endure
And Forgetting What It's Like To Be Clean

My Life, Like A Movie Scene
Played On Re Runs
Over And Over, A Reminder
Of What My Life Was, When It Begun

Please Don't Judge Me, For Being Myself
I Live In A World Where Only I Exist
Get To Know Me Better
Trust Me, My Life, You'd Not Have Missed

I've Handled Rejection, Disappointments
And Truly There's Been Several
Friendships, I Have Loved And Lost
In A Life Distorted, Seems So Very Typical

A Heart So Broken Many Times
I Yearn To Find That Journey, I Truly Belong
Take A Walk In My Shoes
Please Tell Me, My Life Was Not Wrong

WHO I AM

Who Am I, The One That Calms The Oceans
The One That Walks On Water
He, That Gets The Blind To See
That Saves Your Sons And Daughters

Who I Am, The Creator Of Heaven, The Earth
What Is Visible And What Is Never
The One That's Lights The Way
For This Day, Tomorrow And Forever

Many Don't See For Who I Am
Was Betrayed, And Crucified
Jeered By Those, Thought Were Friends
Watched On As My Mother Cried

A Thorny Crown Upon My Head, Was Placed
Lashed Till My Flesh, To The Ground Dripped
Faces Around Me Laughed And Cried
Battered And Bruised My Body Ripped

Who I Am, The One That Will Die For You
So That You May Be Freed
Though You Won't Understand, In
Your Life Of Pride, Lust And Greed

When My Time On Earth Has Come
I Will Resurrect, Then Descend To Walk This Plain
Bringing News Of My Kingdom
And With My Father, Forever I Shall Remain

Here, Angels Trumpet, His Choir Sings
Who I Am, You Will Have Heard
Three Persons In One, Father, Son And Holy Ghost
This Be True, As The Written Word

THE POET

Poems That No-One Gets

To Read, Lie Waste Upon His Book

Shelf

A Failed Writer At The

Mercy Of His

Pen

Scrapped Ideas, Thoughts Jotted

Paper Blotted, Only To Blame

Himself

When Was The Last Meal

If Only He Remembers

When

With Age, He Wonders

Come Fading

Thoughts

At His Desk, Candles

Burnt At Both

Ends

The Nights Are Long

One More Attempt, But Nothing,

Perhaps To Bed As He

Ought

As His Gazed Outside, The Sun, Beyond

The Distance Hills, "I Have To Write"
As Only I, Myself, Can
Depend

The Poet, A Lonely Man

With Nothing But The Passion

To Fulfil A

Dream

His Tools, A Pen, A Quill

And Words, That Hope To

Inspire

A Book, Where Upon

His Shelf Will Sit, A Dollar In His

Pocket, To Build His Self

Esteem

A Small Collection Perhaps,

That Others May Come To

Admire

One Last Attempt, As His

Creative Juices Begin To

Ooze

Thoughts, Starting To Transcend,

Flowing Through The Life Of His

Pen

The View From His Window

A Picturesque Scene, No Time To

Lose

As He Starts, "Escaping Through

The Clouds, The Sun Over The Horizon Sets…"

But Eyes Grow Dim, And It's Back To Bed

Again

THIS IS ME

I'm Not Ashamed Of Who I Am

I Have My Flaws, But This Is
Me

The Scars Of My Past

And I've Live Through
Many

But I Have No Shame, For

This Is Who I
Am

I've Been Haunted By Regrets

Of Those, May've Set Me
Free

Opportunities, I Never Took

My Mistakes, And There Were
Plenty

Help From Friends, I Never Took

Too Busy, To Give A
Damn

Words Once Thrown, Won't Hurt Now

I've Risen Again, This Is
Now

I Won't Hide From The Crowd

Though They've Jeer And
Laughed

They Cannot Break Me, For I Know
That I Am
Strong

And Never, Will I Ever

To Them, Once More
Bow

I Will Sail Through My Perils

Ride Through The Storm, Shall Never Relive My
Past

This World, Will One Day

See, That I Truly
Belong

This Is Me, Hated And Loved, But

I Will Win This Fight, To Carry On This Race I
Live

They Won't Break My Spirit

My Freedom They Cannot
Take

My Belief, My Determination

They Daren't Try
Tame

They Have Hurt Me And Scolded

I Can Forget, But Never
Forgive

Shan't Change The Person I Am -Become

No Apologies To Them I
Make

I Was Raised As How I Am

No Regrets, To Who I
Became

THIS IS ME

TO THE EDGE Of ETERNITY

Vast Worlds Beyond The Cosmos

Beyond The Far Distant

Stars

I'll Follow You To The Edge Of Eternity

Till Our Hearts Will Be As

One

You Entered My Sphere And

Took Me By

Surprise

Could Not Forget That Impression

You Stamped In My Heart

And Left It In

Scars

And It Was In That Moment Of Time

My Affection You Had

Won

A Glimmer, A Sparkle

A Radiance Emerged From Your

Eyes

To The Edge Of Eternity,

If Such A Place, May So

Exist

I Know Deep Down Within

Our Hearts Bears No

Distance

No Space, Nor Time, Can
Ever Come Between
Us
We'll Be Together Forever
Till The End Of Time
Permits
To Be Bound By Grace
That Our Body, Our Minds May
Listen
To Travel Down Life's Roads
Knowing You Are Worthy Of My
Trust
To The Edge Of Eternity

THE MIRROR

Upon The Mantle Piece It Stands
With A Golden Rim, And Ancient Did It Appear
Spherically Cracked And Tarnished
The Baroque Era Or Such That Year

Dim And Dusty In A Room Barely Lit
Cept For The Rays Crept In From The Cracks
The Mirror, Its History Of The Bygone Era
There's Nothing In This Room But Black

Turning On The Lamp
There It was, Staring Right At Me
It's The Reflection Of Who I Am
Or Was, Was All That I Could See

A Cold And Ominous Shiver Ran Down My Spine
Something Sinister, Something Wicked
To Me, It Was Talking Back
A Ghostly Apparition, Why Me Had It Picked

Fear In Me Spiralled
As I Looked Into The Mirror's Face
Was This The Person That I'll Become
And That I, Have Fallen From Grace

Was This Mirror A Journey Into
My Future Or My Past
An Eerie Coldness Filled The Room
Upon The Cobwebbed Walls, Shadows Cast

The Mirror Is Just An Illusion
A One-Dimensional Timeless Plane
Reflecting Images Of The Things To Come
And Things I Could Not Explain

I Closed My Eyes, And Hoped
That This Was All Just A Dream
As I Began To Open Them
Wanting To Shout Out And Scream

What Stared Gazing Back At Me
In This Looking Glass, A Reflection
Was I To Believe This Was Real
Or An Elaborate Hoax Or Deception

The Image Within That Mirror Flickered
Distorted Voices Echoing Again And Again
It Has No Soul With No Emotions
This Torture, One I Cannot Pretend

A Maniacal Laughter Bellowed Out
"I've Come For You, Your Time Is Up"
Like Something The Grim Reaper Might Moan
And Dare Not, Him, Disrupt

Looking Closer Into The Mirror
His Eyes Were Glowing, A Burning Red
Flares Shooting At Me
Still His Evil Spread

It Can't Hurt Me, I Think
I Must Release From Its Clutches
To Escape From Whatever
It Is, That It Touches

The Laughter, Embedded In My Psyche
Etching Away My Cognition
I'm Unable To Think Or Speak At All
I Might Just Surrender Into Submission

Without Warning, Skeletal Hands
Lunging Out, Grabbing At My Throat
Nails, Like Talons, With Flesh Off The Bone
Near And Near It Had Approached

With No Time To Think, Acted Instinctively
And Freed Myself From Its Vice Like Grip
Gasping For Air As Saliva Dribbled To My Face
Had Only One Chance, Then, Its Hands Did Slip

But Not Without A Fight
The Mirror Now Broken To Fragmented Pieces
Scattered Beyond Repair
Must Work Fast Before My Paranoia Increases

What An Episode, Like Death Had Warmed Up
Or Something Out Of A Horror Movie
You Wouldn't Read About It
But It Really Happened, Thinking Kinda Spooky

Sunlight Set In, In That Once Dusky Room
As I Drew Back The Drapes
A Sense Of Relief Set Over Me
Felt Entrapped When I Thought Was No Escape

TEN THOUSAND REASONS

I Cannot Think One Reason Why I
Love You Not, But Ten Thousand, Why I
Do
The Way Your Hair Glistens
When The Sun, Upon It
Shines
Your Selfless Kindness
When The Morning You Greet With A
Smile
Your Readiness To Forgive
When The Troubles I Put You
Through
When I Look Into Your Eyes
Reminds Me What Your Love
Defines
Ten Thousand Reasons, My
Love For You's Been Worth The
While
Ten Thousand Reasons, Birds
Sing On The First Day Of
Spring
Just Like A Fairytale Story
From A Child's Nursery
Book

They Come To See You, Gathering

Roses From The

Fields

Just Like Those Birds,

Joy And Happiness To Me You

Bring

I Will Cherish You, The Morning

The Nights, Every Day, However You

Look

Ten Thousand Reason I'd Follow

Whatever Days Bring, Whatever

They May

Yield

Ten Thousand Reasons Id

Never Leave You

Hurting

Many More, To Never Leave You

Alone And

Crying

You're The Essence That

Breathes Life Into

Me

The More I Think Of You

A Life Together, Would Be

Certain.

If I Said I Didn't Mean It
Honey, This I Would Be
Lying
Ten Thousand Reasons
For You And I To
Be
You, I, Can Withstand The Perils,
What Life Has To
Offer
The Good Times And Bad
When Moments Pass Our
Ways
When You're Sick, I'll Be There
When In Doubt, There To Make Things
Certain
You And I Will Be There, Now And
For Always, For Each
Other
By Your Side, Never Out Of Sight
To One Day Hope, A Family We'll
Raise
I Will Cherish You Always
Till Our Lives Draw Its Final
Curtain
And Then Truly, I'd Have Loved
You Eternally For More Than
A Thousand
Reasons

THE LAST CHAPTER

When You Were Born, This Was The

First Of Many

Pages

Many Will Be Written, Of

The Stories That Will Be

Told

Your Life, As In Those Pages, Were

Labelled And

Numbered

You Were Born And Nurtured

With A Smile.

Contagious

Your Eyes Lit Up, In A

Shining Glimmer Like

Gold

Your Endeavours To Walk, Effortless,

Fell, But Then You

Conquered

Turning Over The Pages

The Years Flew Past

By

God Had Authored Your Life,

Guiding You Through

Time

Decisions To Be Made, You
Learnt From No
Book
You Never Gave Up The Chase
And Never Wondered
Why
Obstacles, There Were Many
But, Those Mountains You Did
Climb
You Made A Home, A Family Too
Did For Them, Whatever It
Took
It's The Last Chapter, Your Time
Is Near
Complete
You've Lived A Life Fulfilled
With All That You've Been
Through
Amongst The Many Heartaches
And Grievous
Sorrows
You Looked Life In The Eye And
Never Backed Down, Or Accepted
Defeat
That's Why God Gave Us Angels
And Why He Gave Us
You

It's The Last Chapter, This Book Of Your Life

Turning Back The Pages

So, Will Never Be The

End

When The Time To Leave Us Is Here

And Your Body, Is One With

Earth

We'll Look Back On Those Pages

And Time Reading, We'll

Spend

TODAY I'M PUSHING BACK

He Wore My Ring, When We Shared Our Vows
Before Friends And Family, God, The Divine
Those Were Our Sacraments Pledged To Keep
In Our Love That We Defined

In Sickness And In Health
For Richer Or Poorer, To These We Agreed
To Honour And Cherish
If This Love is To Succeed

But Those Years Dwindled, Wasted Away
Now We Are Barely Friends
We Don't Even Talk Anymore
No Time With Me, Does He Spend

In The Same House, Like Strangers
Who Have Never Met
Conversations Just Died
He Sees Right Through Me No Attention I Get

Only When He Wants Something
Does He Speak
Or When It's In The Bedroom
Favours He Seeks

No Roses, Birthdays Or Valentines
Or Any Efforts To Show His Love
He Has No Ideas As
To What I'm Thinking Of

Besides My Bed, A Photo Of That Wedding Day
Torn In The Middle, Over An Argument We Had
I Tried To Resurrect Those Moments
But Only Tears Did I Shed

Am I Not Pretty Enough
A Bad Wife Or Mother
I Gave Him All That I Could
Perhaps It's Time To Find another

I Was His Subject Of Abuse And Torment
When He Had One Of His Moody Turns
Till He Broke Me Down In Tears
He Left Me With Bruises And Burns

But Today I Am Pushing Back
To That Reminder Of His Hate
Accidents, He Will Call Them
But Honey, Your Apologies Are Just Too Late

But It Was Out Of Spite And Malice
I Married A Monster I Came To Realize.
It's Not Too Late To Back Away
From His Fury, Or Whatever May Arise

Never Again, Will He Hurt Me
Or Watch Me Cry
For Today I Am Pushing Back
And All I Can Do, Is Try

I Will Count My Blessing
And To The Future, Walk With Pride
No Reason To Stay Here, In This Living Hell
This Infernal Emotional Ride

Like A Roller Coaster, I Will Get Off
And Keep Looking Forward
The Future, Is In My Grasp
Step By Step, I'll Be Searching Onward

Wiping My Slate Clean,
Recollections Of Him, I'll Never To Relive
No Haunting Memories
And To His Actions, I Will Never Forgive

I Will Sail, To The Horizon
Where The Sun Meets The Sea
Away From The Misery
And Then, Shall I Be Set Free

That Will Be The Day That I Pushed Back
From All That I Had Endured
And My Identity I Will Restore
To Find Comfort As I Deserve, I Should

No More Will I Bow Down To Any Man
But Only To God On That Judgement Day
Always Heard My Pleas
Saw When I Was Down, Never Turned Me Away

Brought Me From The Pits Of Darkness
Took Me In His Arms, Gave Me Refuge
My Dear Child, I Saw When You Were Hurt
His Love, He Would Never Refuse

I Believed I Lost The Will To Love
And Thought To Never Be Loved Again
I Met This Man, That Rocks My World
Has Restored My Faith In Men

He Knows What I'm Thinking.
Or When Im Hurting, In Pain
Could He Be The One And Be My World?
Or With Him For Life I Will Remain?

He Was A Boy I Used To Know
And With Me, A Photo I Did Carry
I'm Certain He Will Have Me
Perhaps Too, Will Come To Marry

He Knew What A Woman Wanted
Nothing Was Much To Ask
Treated Me Kindly, I Was His Only One
And Like A Few, He Never Wore A Mask

He's On My Mind, Every Waking Hour
I Can Feel His Heartbeat Again My Chest
Though He Is Not With Me
Am I Really Feeling This?

Today I Am Pushing Back
But How Can I, When He Is So Sweet
Says The Right Words, As If He Knew Me
He Would Make My Life Complete

Just The Other Day Roses, He Would Send
Not Even Valentines, Or Anything Special
Was Just Because He Could
And Told Him, Perhaps One Days We'd Settle

His Heart I Felt So Precious
I Knew With The Feelings He Shared
When He Spoke I Nearly Fainted
His Charm, Was All I Knew He Cared

He Had Me Hypnotise That Very Day
Is This Really Happening
When I Thought It Would Never
And I Was Only Really Imagining

Had Love Deserted Me, And Now
Making A Comeback
Or Perhaps I Have Been Smitten
And Have Been Thrown Off Track

Is This My Fairytale Come True
As In A Bedtime Story
When The Prince, His Maiden Meets
And Together They Will Rise In Glory

Where To The Far Distance Sunset
On A Horse They Will Ride
Then She Will Await That Day
She Will Become His Bride

STANDING ROOM ONLY

The Night Was Long
The Music Blaring
Loud
In The Bar Room
Smoke Filled The
Air
Standing Room Only
For This Restless
Crowd
Your Thoughts You Couldn't
Hear, Anybody Really
Care?
Men, In A Drunken Stupor
The Musty, Beer Scented
Smells Upon Their
Shirts
Women, No Better Off
Parade In Some Low Cut
Tops
Slurred Speech, Men's Hands
Roaming Above Their
Skirts
Ogling Eyes, Sizing Up
And Down, Men's Jaw
Drops

Standing Room Only
Shoving, Pushing Toe
Stomping
The Lights Dimmed,
Music, To The Ears
Heightened
No Sign Of Easing Off
Or Even The Thought Of
Stopping
Standing Before Him In A
Black Dress And Shapely, His Moods
Enlightened
He Spies Her From Across
The Room, No Notice She
Takes
Dodging Drunken Bodies
To Get To Her, If Given Half A
Chance
A Smile He Shares, Trembling
Voice, No Sound He
Makes
The Band, Playing Jiving
Tunes, No One Got Up To
Dance
"Would You Like To…"
"What?" "Oh Sorry, To Dance"
"Oh, Okay"

"Can Hardly Move In
Here" Standing Room
Only
"Then, Would You Like To
Sit As They
Play"
"Or Go Across The
Street, For A Coffee, Take Things
Slowly
"No I Like It Here, 'Cept, For
That Sign," Standing Room
Only
"I Often Come Here, But
Never This
Packed"
I Sometimes Come Here
When I Am Down Or
Lonely
And Hope It's A Beautiful
Woman, I've Come To
Attract
"I Haven't Seen You Here Before"
No! I Am New In This
Town"
"Do You Live Locally
Around These
Parts

"No! Not Really, I
Tend To Move
Around"
But Would Often Come
Here, When, The Summer
Starts
"It's Hard To Dance, When
Standing Room Only, Can I Buy You A
Drink"
"Well! That's Mighty Fine
Thank You, So
Kind"
"I Don't Know What To
Have, What Do You
Think"
"A Cocktail Mixture, I'd
Hope You'll Like And Won't
Mind"
The Early Morning Closes In
A Scuffle, Bottles, Fists
Flying
"Can We Leave This Joint"
Afraid Someone'll Get
Hurt
"No Place For A Lady
Such As You, There Ain't No
Denying"

"You're So Considerate. No Man
Ever I Met. Trust Me, I've
Searched"
"I'll Drive You Home If You
Would Like Me
To"
"That Is So Generous
Of You Once
Again
"It Is No Bother, Want
To Get You Home, Besides
I Really Do Like
You"
I'm Harry By The Way,
And You, Oh! I'm
Madeleine"

MY UNIVERSE

You'll Always Be My Universe
Even If Worlds From The Outer Plains Explode
Into A Myriad Fragmented Pieces
Nothing Be Taken Away, Of How They Once Glowed

No Place I'd Rather Be Than
To Share The Cosmos, And Every Galaxy With You
Where Nothingness Exist
But Together We Will Pull Through

The Other Day, Woke Up In Cold Sweat
Dreamt Our Worlds Had Collided
I Search For You, But Not To Be Found
I Scoured The Earth, Unguided

It Was The Thought Of You
That Propelled Me To Live
And If Ever I Wasn't With You
Please Find In Your Heart To Forgive

Every Night I Gaze The Heavens
And Wondering Where You Are
Somewhere Out There
Beyond That Reachable Star

I Knew My Universe Was Out There
And Soon Enough I'll Be A Part Of It
Amongst The Stars, Where I'll Find You
And Never Shall I Quit

Eyes Glisten, When The Star Light
Hits Upon Your Eyes
That Smile, When You Wear That Translucent Gloss
Your Beauty, I Found, To Mesmerize

But Nothing Can Take Away
The Stars That Brightly Shine
In The Darkness, And The Wind
Calling Out Your Name To Be Mine

My Universe, You Were Destined To Be
The Never-Ending, The Eternal Infinite
In An Endless Oceans Of Stars
We Are An Instant Hit

When I Looked In Your Eyes
Time Seems To Stand Still
And Sands, From An Hour Glass Slowly Slip
Until One Day It Will Again Fill

Every Minute I Am Not With You
Time Robs Me Blindly
Taking Away What Could Make Me Whole
And Every Day, Is There To Remind Me

My Universe Is Not Limited By Time
In An Ever-Increasing Realm
A Realm We Cannot Perceive
Or Pretend To Live In Them

But I Know, I Shall One Day Live In Yours
To Build Our Own
To Wake Up Next To You
And Never Feel Alone

UNWRITTEN

I Sit And Wonder Of What Next To Write
But All I Hear, Mere Scrambled Thoughts
My Pen, snuggly In Hand
Waiting For The Words To Come Across

Inspirations, Longing To Emerge
But All That Remains Are Visions Unwritten
Pages Before Me Left Blank, Unscripted
Ideas And Notions Left Hidden

Out Of Mind, Waiting, An Inspiration To Write
Scrunched Up Papers, Basket To The Brim
Tossed, With Words, Upon Them Scribbled
This Poet's Chances Are Looking Slim

Words Unwritten, longing To Evolve
No Patience, May Give Up The Ghost
But I Must Continue, Persevere
It's The Love For Writing, I Love The Most

A Surge, An Impulse Like A Lightening Volt
Came Over My Body, Sweeping
Resembling A Magician, How From Nothing
Words Came Leaping

Ink Blots Thereon My Page, Splattered,
Upon The Few Notes Scrawled
What Was Once Unwritten
Is Now A Poem Near Formed

It's Not Much To Look At
I Know You Would Probably Agree
But A Page That Was Unwritten,
Hope Interested You, To Some Degree

It Was A Long Time In Coming
I Hope You've Been Truly Amazed
I Really Was Only Joking
There Are No Words, However You Gazed

For The Words, Still Remain Unwritten
No Thoughts Came To Surface
No Vibes Electrified In Me
I Cannot Therefore Publish, For This Purpose

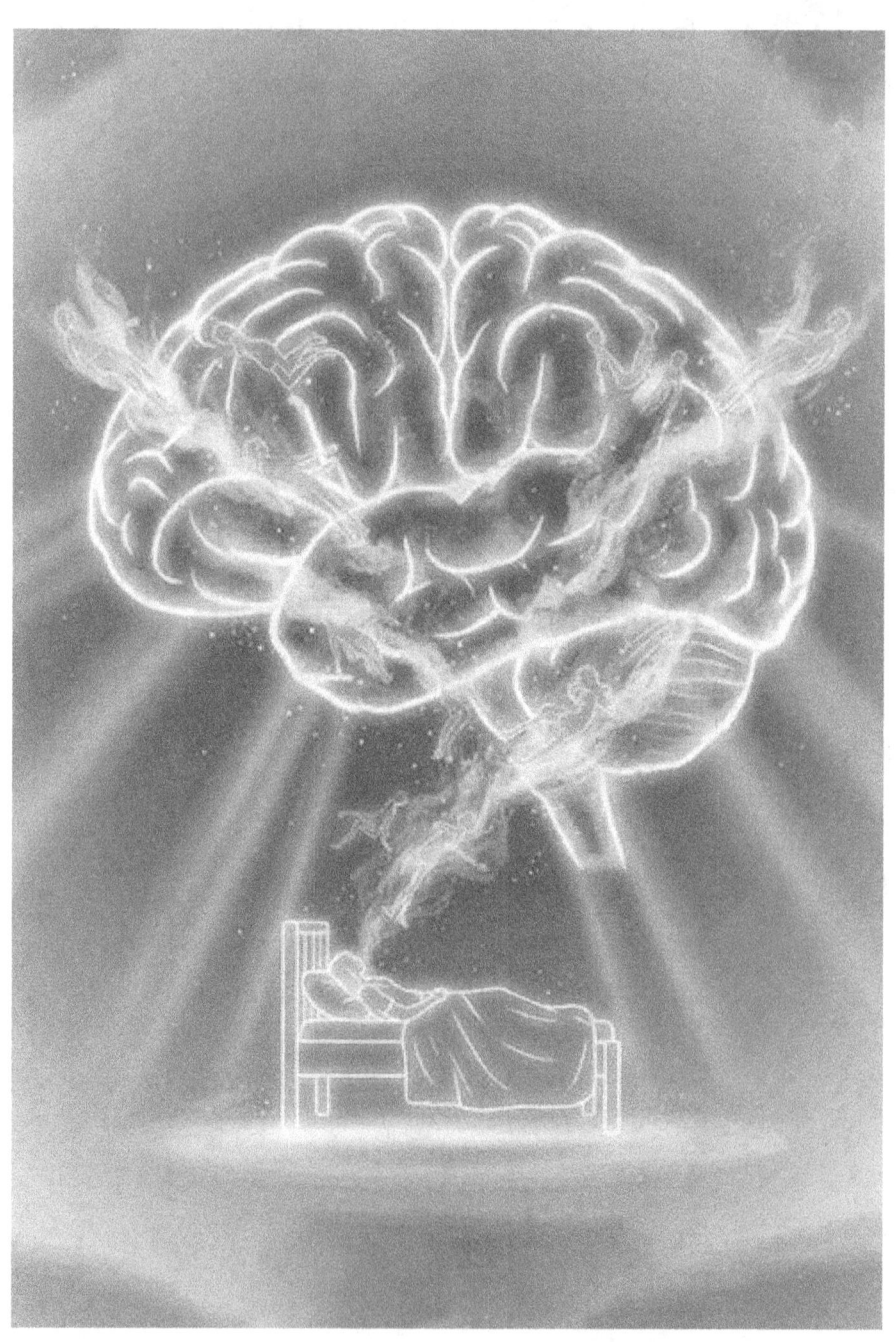

RECURRING DREAMS

From Dawn Till Dusk, The Night Creeps,

To My Bed, I Must Go And

Lay

What Stories Will Fill My Head

What Dreams Will I

Encounter

Are These The Tales

So Far Not Yet

Told

As They Eat Away My

Conscious Mind, What Message

Will Be

Conveyed

I Cannot Make Out These

Recurring Dreams, All Just A

Blur

Like A Story- Tale, Episodes,

Slowly Begin To

Unfold

Recurring Dreams Of Visions

Realistically, Vivid, What Do They

Mean

I Am Floating, I Am Falling

I Am Startled In

Confusion

You Are There To Ease Troubles

To Catch Me When I

Fall

Like Something Out Of

A Movie Heroine

Scene

Is This Real, Dreams Can Appear That Way

Or Maybe A Case Of

Delusion

In These Dreams Recurring

Can You Hear Me When I

Call

Recurring Dreams, Nightmarish

Haunting, I Feel My Chest

Collapse

Gasping For Air, A Cold

Sweat, Leaving Me

Drenched

Wake Up, Wake Up, Telling Myself

These Demons Of Dreams Wont

Allow

Maybe I'm Destined To Live

Out These Illusions,

Perhaps

But The Fear Instilled Within

Leaving Me In A Fisted

Clench

Wondering Now, To
Arise From This, But
How
I Pray To God That I Awaken,
To Take Away These Recurring
Dreams
Perhaps Be All Forgotten
And Setting Them
Aside
After all, Dreams Are Fantasies
And Nothing As They
Seem
A Manifestation, What's In Your
Head, Or Hiding Deep
Inside

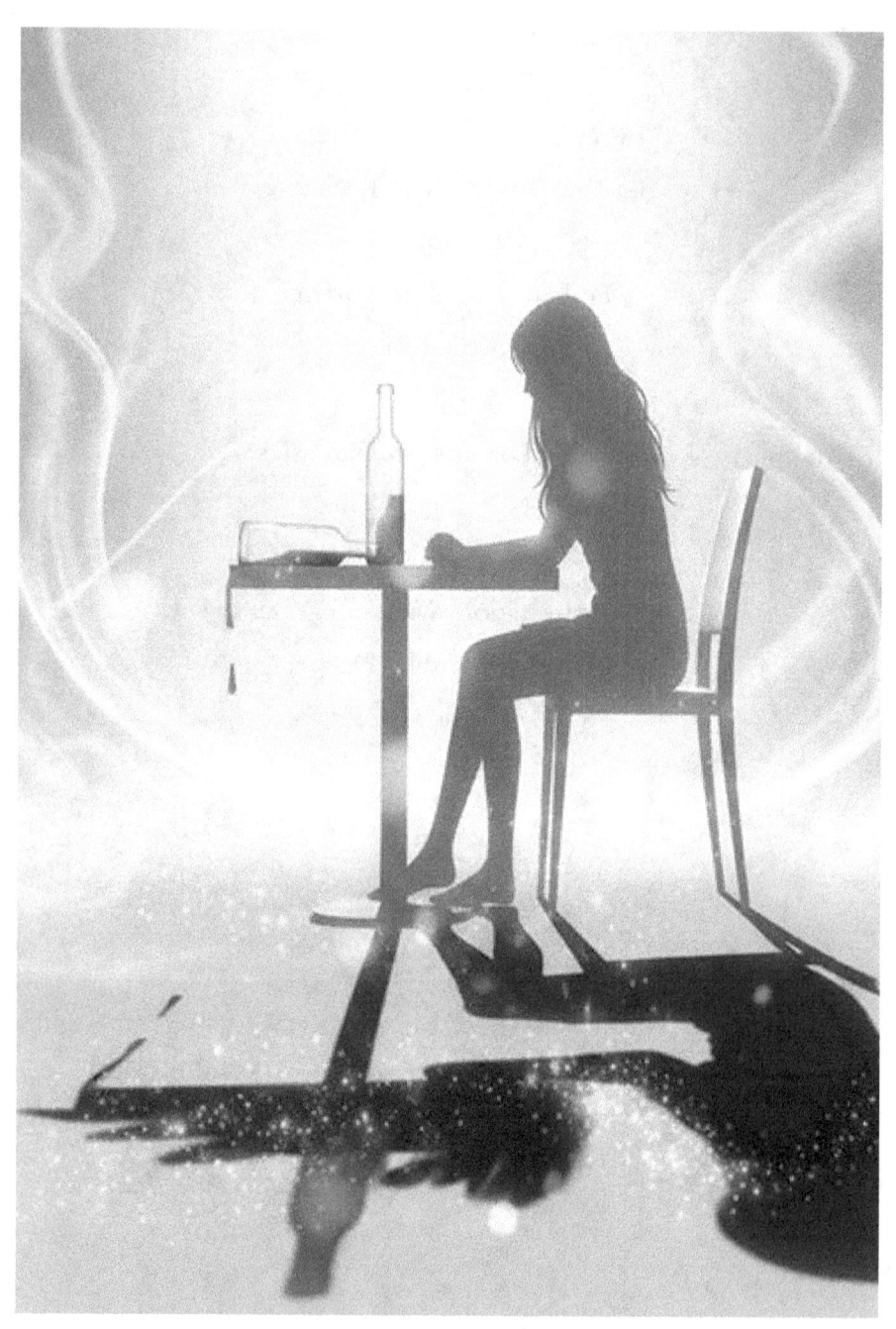

A BOTTLE AND ME

A Cry For Help But No One Listened
He Wasn't Coming Back, Left Me For Another
The Best Years I Had Given Him
Now His Love, For The Other

I Have No Reasons For This Life
I'm Just A Wasted Space
My Thoughts Don't Seem My Own
No Control, I Don't Belong In This Place

A Bottle And Me, Will Make Good Friends
Drink It All Night, Won't Feel A Thing
Perhaps It'll End It All
And Eternal Peace It Will Bring

This Pisco, For A Special Occasion
Sorry It Had Come To This
But No One To Love Me, Or To Hug
Doubt, If I'll Ever Be Missed

Razor Blade In Hand, Daring Myself
Voices In My Head "Do It, Won't Hurt A Bit
Trembling To Hold It Tight
"Do It Now, Or Might As Well Quit"

These Voices Pound Within Me
I'm Going To End It All, Will He Even Care?
Or Say, "Don't To Do It"
Maybe Even Slightly, Shed A Tear

A Bottle And Me, Is All I Need
Nothing Will Hurt, Nothing At All
Do It Quick, One Slash
Feeling Trapped Behind this emotional Wall

If Death Comes Knocking, Will Let Him In
Take Me And Ease This Pain
My Heart's Been Broken, Too Many Times
No Reasons On Earth, I Should Remain

"My Children, Who'll Look After Them?"
I Must Be Strong, They Are The Spirit Within
I Might Not Have Him, I've Accepted That
Can Never Be, As It Had Been

A Bottle And Me, A friend You Cannot Divide
With Me, Through This Difficult Moment
As, Despair Came Over Me
And it was this bottle, that had spoken

So, I'll End It All, this I Must
Is There Another Way That I Can Find?
My Head's Made Up, It's What I Know
Or Perhaps Just Losing My Mind

Tell My Kids I Love Them Sincerely
Shall I Not Awaken From This Slumber
I'll Be There Always In Their Prayers
Need Never Have To Wonder

How To Restore A Shattered Glass
As My Life Has Been, Has No Purpose, Has No Use
Piece By Piece It Can Be Restored
But How Can The Emotional Abuse?

If He Loved Me, He'd Have Stayed
But Chose To Leave For Someone Better
Was She Richer, Prettier, Smarter Than Me?
I Cannot Say, I Never Met Her

To The World I Might Leave Behind, I Am Sorry
You Cannot Comprehend My Sadness
That Bottle And Me Headed, For A One-Way Ticket
Perhaps There Is Light, Maybe Darkness

I Can Survive This, No Other better Option
Stand On My Own Too Feet,
Will Kick That Bottle To The Curb
And Hope My Life Will Be Complete

NEVER ENOUGH

I Wanted You All, But All, You Couldn't Give
You Gave Me Your Ring, But Was Never Enough
A House A Roof, The Fancy Clothes
I Wanted More, But All You Gave Me, Was Stuff

A Commitment To Be With Me
To Live Out Our Lives Together
The Promise To Cherish And To Love
Till The End Of Our Days Forever

It Was Never Enough, To Give You A Child
To Start A Family Or Our Own
You Had Things To Do, But Not With Me
Parties With The Boys. Left Me Home Alone

You Said It Would Only Be A Few Hours
But I Stayed Up And Waited For You
I Called, But You Never Answered
Do U Realise, What You Put Me Through

It Was Never Enough, That I Took You Back
Yes! You Said That You Were Sorry
But How Can I Now Believe Such Words
When, Next Time, Will Be The Same Old Story

I Held My Breath, And Bit My Tongue
I Wanted So Much To Believe You Were Real
How Can I Forgive, This Sense Of Betrayal?
Do You Even Know, How I Might Even Feel

Darling! I Cannot Go On Like This
I Wanted More, But You Were Never Enough
I Cannot Stop Thinking That,
It Wasn't Me You Were Thinking Of

Maybe Our Parting Ways Is Best For Us
We Can Be Friends And Perhaps Start Over
So Much To Explore, How To Make This Work
I'm Sure In Time, Will Bring Us Closer

Was It Maybe Me, That Was Never Enough?
I Put The Blame On You, For The Things
I Couldn't Handle, Being With You
I Realise Now, It's Your Presence That Love Brings

MY REDEEMER KING

I Have Lived Through Many
Dangers That Life Hurled Me
Through
Your Calming Voice I Followed
When In The Depth Of
Despair
You Are My Redeemer King
Whose Love Within Me
Grew
You Stood By Me When In
Troubled Times And To You
My Soul I'd
Bare
In The Sea Of Doubt, When
I Ventured Alone, It Was
Your Arms I Felt Around
Me
A Feeling Of Such Warmth,
Secured By Your Love
Devine
You Lifted Me Up, My Spirit
Ascended, Heaven Bound
There Be Set
Free

In Awe Of Its Beauty,

In All That We See, In Your Worldly

Design

My Life, Once Miniscule

By Your Vast

Creation

A Lonely Subject Chained

By Insecurities Left Me Helpless,

Misguided

You Rendered Your Kindness

Granted Upon Me,

Salvation

You Led Me Through

The Storms, When The Wind, Rain

Subsided.

When You Said "You Are My Son"

You Freed Me From The Fires Of

Hell

Then, No Darkness Shall I Fear

No Pains Would I

Bear

And In Your Castles

Above The Clouds, With You, I Will

Dwell

And There Through Eternity,

To Live With You

There

A WORLD

Imagine You Could Travel
Travel To A World Of The Imagination
Beyond The Realm Of Reality
No Need For Reasons Or Explanation

Where Unicorn's Flight Above The Clouds
And Fairies Sprinkle Their Dust
In A Land Of Fantasy
Where Illusions You Can Trust

A Backdrop Scene Of Colours
Cascading, With Ripples In A Pond
Your Reflection Into Another World
Deeper Deeper, Far Beyond

Live In A World Where Wishes Do Come True
One Minute You're Flying
Then Sliding A Rainbow To Its Gold
With Only Happiness, Laughter, And Love Undying

Take Me To A World, One, Not Of This Kind
Where Giants, Big As Trees, Gently They Roam
Through Prairies, Fields And Plains
A Fictitious Land, They Call Their Home

There, I Am The Main Attraction
Like The Comic Book Hero
Saving The Damsel In Distress
And Lives Again To Save Another, Tomorrow

In This Never-Never Land Of Make Believe
A World Of Dragons And Wizards
And Castles Upon A Mountain Top
Where Lives The Magic Of Sorcery And Witches

Molten Lava Of Gold Runs Through This Land
In This Fairyland, Your Dreams Are Real
For When You Awaken They Cease To Exist
But In Your Mind, No One Can Steal

I'll Show You A World,
Where All You Believe Is No Illusion
Where Your Dreams, Become The Undreamt
And Your Mind, Sets Free From Confusion

Would You Like To Travel, To A World Of Imagination
Where Nothing Is Impossible
You Will Be A King, A Ruler
Where Fiction, Is Made Possible

If Only, Yes If Only

AFTER THE FIRE

It Was An Early Autumn's Day
That Much, To This Day I Recalled
Not A Breeze, Not Even A Sound
Only The Wind, My Name It Called

Thought Nothing Of It
And Went About On My Way
The Sky Clouded Over All Around,
Black And Eerie, It Was That Day

Something Ominous, An Awkward Feeling
You Know, That Gut Instinct
The One You Can't Shake Up
But That Feeling, Was Very Distinct

Nothing Like I Have Ever Felt Before
And Will Soon Be Revealed
In A Distance, Miles Outs
Beyond The Yonder Fields

The Sky Lit Up With Flying Embers
Like Fireflies, Chasing The Flickering Flames
Children Screaming, Families Running
"My God" One Woman Exclaims

Saving What Little They Possessed
Before All Turned To Dust
And After The Fire, All Be Lost
Would Have To Adapt, To Readjust

After The Fire, When You
All You Can Do, Fall To Your Knees
And Pray That Memories Can Be Salvaged
That Moment, Your Mind Could Not Be Eased

Watching In Fear, Overcome With Distress
Where To Start, Who Will Assist
Questions With No Answers
All Around You, People In The Midst

Retrieving What Little They Can.
Houses In Rubbles, Up In Smoke
Crazy To Think, Started From Nothing
Seemed Like A Dream, And From It, You Woke

They Prayed For The Rains, To Bring Reprieve
But Dismally Never Came
And Before Their Eyes, All That Be
Standing, Was The Houses' Wooden Frames

After The Fire, When All That's Left
Are The Scattered Ashes
The Memories Remain Long Buried
The Fields, With Their Burnt-Out Patches

After The Fire, Looking Back Then
Lives Can Never Be Restored
They Live On To Other Days
But Still Those Days, Could Never Be Ignored

It Was An Early Autumn's Day
That Much, To This Day I Recalled
Not A Breeze, Not Even A Sound
Only The Wind, My Name It Called

THE DAY THE COLOURS FADED

Echoes In The Hallway Sounded,
The Day, The Colours Faded
When Their Smiles Turned Into Frowns
Their Enthusiasm Drew Jaded

The Vibrant Hues Upon
Their Faces Had Disappeared
Not A Whisper, Not A Sound
When All At Once, All Hope Was Cleared

The Song Of The Chirping Robins
Beyond These Walls Receded
Clouds Up Above, An Ominous Sight
One More Chance At Life, All They Needed

The Day The Colours Faded
Not A Symphony Was Heard
The Air Was Muted With The Woeful Cries
All That Remains Now, Are Their Pleas Unheard

When Their World Was Once Lit Up
With The Glory And Joys Of Life,
Now Darkness Looms In Sight
And Fear With Hatred, Set In Their Eyes

These Of The Residents That
Paced The Once Crowded Hallways
But Now, Just Empty Corridors
From The Bygone, Endless Days

They Walked With Shackles
Clanging Around Their Feet
Straight Jacketed Like Criminals
Here They Were Met With Defeat

With Mouth Drooling In Their Saliva
Eyes Rolled Back, Looking Into An Empty Space
Heavily Dosed With A Lethal Concoction
With Anguish Etched Upon Each Face

Heads Shaven With A Ten Inch Incision
Blood Freshly Trickling Upon Their Brow
Under The Knife, Like Some Lab Rat
Death, They Wished Upon, If Only They'd Allow

The Day The Colours Faded
When Blood Stained The Walls
In The Asylum For The Criminally Insane
No Longer Now, Do They Roam The Halls

With Grime Plastered In Every Corner
Dented Walls From A Fisted Rage
Roaches Prowling Awaiting Feed,
Scarpering To Every Cage

Patients Dragging Their Feet
To Escape Their Confines
Freedom Comes At A Cost
An Escape Route, What They Hope To Find

They Look At Me For A
Chance To Flee, Reaching At Me To Grab
But Side Stepped Away
Narrowly Missing, Being Stabbed

Outside These Walls
Fences, Barricaded And Barbed
No Getting Out, Die If You Dare Try
By Sharpshooter On Guard

The Laughter Once Echoed
Before That Day Colours Faded
A Glow In Their Eyes Back Then
All That Exists, Is A Life Degraded

Their Life, Within A Padded Cell
Where Windows Are Barred
A Cut Out, Where Food's Collected
Longing To Be Freed Beyond The Outside Yard

That Was Then, Before The Colours Faded
Now Closed For Decades
Still, You Can Hear Their Screams
I Am Old, But Still Recall Those Days

I Hear That One Fled
And Was Never Seized
A Search Party Scoured The Plains
The Local Paper Did Read

With Bitterness I Dodged To Recall
The Lives Tragically Taken
When Experimented On
Put To Sleep, Never To Awaken

I Was The Doctor, A Surgeon
Sought Out To Find, A Cure
For Mental Illness
But Practice Back Then, Seemed Unsure

PARENTHOOD

It All Starts In A Twinkling Of Their Eyes
Boy Meets Girl In The Park
Or At The Beach Perhaps
But A Journey Together In Life, They Will Embark

Pretty Soon, They Get To Know Each Other
Hold Hands, Sharing Their Most Precious Secrets
Their Strong Points, Their Bad And
Their Innermost Weakness

Their Trust Is Taken To The Next Level
Talking About The Long Term Together
A Future, Building A Home, Perhaps Marriage
He Must Build His Courage, A Way To Ask Her

A Star Shoots Across The Sky
They Engage In Bodily Affection
Chemistry Building Up Inside
Then Suddenly Conception

Now It's A Waiting Game For The Pair
To Starts A New Generation, Be It A Girl Or A Boy
Nine Months Will Pass Before Their New Creation
And Moments Throughout, They Will Enjoy

The Father, With The Pleasure Of Cutting
The Newborn's Umbilical Cord
As It Takes Its First Breath of Life
They are Thankful, For God's Creative Reward

The Wait Is Over, They Are Received Into Parenthood
Welcoming The Birth Of Their Child
Whom They'll Raise And Nurture, As Countless Before
Taking First Photos Of The Day It Smiled

Adapting To Her Maternal Instincts
She Opens Her Nursing Bra, To Seem Discreet
The Baby Latches On And Finds Its Sucking Rhythm
Mum Carefully Watches, As Her Darling Eats

With Its Life And Existence
Now Comes, Their Parenthood Obligation
They Will Name Giving it An Identity
On A "Naming Day" Celebration

The Baby's First Sounds It Hears
Whilst It Gazes Upon Its New Parents
Taking Home For The First Time
After Mum's Nine Months Of Endurance

With parenthood, the responsibilities
Of the nappy changing ritual
Mum and dad, sharing the pleasure
This agreement is mutual

As The Child Starts To Grow
Ever So Learning, And The Hearing Of Sounds
Images That Will Sure To Enlighten
And Parents Will Be Teaching It, Its Bounds

At Around Ten Months, Sometimes Earlier
Starting To Crawl, Picking Things
Testing It's Oral Stimulation
Now Parenthood Will Seriously Begin

The Joys Of Parenthood
Is Not Limited To The Child's Feeding
Being Spoon Fed, To Satisfy Its Hunger
And Independent Eating

Mouth Smeared With Pureed Food
All Over Their Tray, Pasting Everything
Then Time To Burp, Over The Shoulders
Lo And Behold A Projectile Of Food, When Puking

Then Comes The Bathing, Both Mum And Dad
Share In The Excitement Of Being Splashed
But The Baby Is Having Fun, But Soon His
His Nappy And Talc, To Prevent From Any Skin Rash

Crying During Early Morning Hours
They Cannot Quite Figure The Reasons
Feeding Doesn't Seem To Work
So Consults The Books And Figure It's Teething

Parenthood And The Proud Moments
Lack Of Sleep, For The Poor Mum
Dad, Can't Hear A Thing
Or Maybe Just Playing Dumb

He Starts Early For Work, Needs His Sleep
He Is A Young Father, So Money He Needs
In Raising And Supporting This Family
And If He Is To Succeed

The Joys Of Parenthood
Witnessing His Child's First Baby Walk
Falling Many Times, Then Getting Up
Babbling Baby Words, Trying To Talk

His First Tooth Starts To Emerge
But Still Surviving On Pureed Foods
His Attitudes Begin To Change
From His Other Tempers To His Bitter Moods

Sometimes Though, A Little Pat On His Behind
Setting The Rules, So To Correct
In Time, Yes Will Understand
Might Even Earn These Parents, Respect

As New To Parenthood, They Are Faced With
The Challenges Of Making Time
With Communication Along The Way,
Playing Role Models, when Esteem Will Climb

Importantly Of All, Cherish Their Lives
And Showing Unconditional Affection
With Discipline But Fairness
As You Point Them, In The Right Direction

BEAUTIFUL IN WHITE

From That Very Instance That
My Eyes Laid Upon You
I Knew We Were Meant For Each Other
How Much I Love You, If Only You Knew

I Know You Couldn't See That
Being Shy, You Blushed And Turned Away
I Chased Behind To Take Your Hand
I Recall Those Days, As If It Was Yesterday

We Spoke Awhile, I Earned Your Trust
And Days Turned To Months, To Years
We Spoke Of Wedding Bells, Horses, Carriages
Your Eyes Aglow, As Your Face Filled With Happy Tears

Looking At Your Eyes Weep
Became So Nervous, Wanted To Ask For Your Hand
In That Special Moment, Thought You'd Have Run
And If You Did, Then I'd Understand

It Was Every Woman's Dream To Marry
Walking Down The Aisle, Beautiful In White
With A Prince, By Her Side
To Shower Her With A Love That Will Ignite

I Envisioned The Future,
And You Look Beautiful In Golden Curls
A Bouquet Of Flowers And Ribboned Hair
Your Dressed Adorned In Pearls

I Knew I Found You, My One And Only
Like A Puzzle, You Were My Missing Piece
Now That I Have You, I Want To Tell You
That Within Me, I Have Found Peace

And From This Day Forward
Till My Life Has Ceased To Exist
You Will Always Have My Heart, My Spirit
Please Know, It Is You, I Will Have Missed

You're The Very Reason, I Stand Before You
Just Want To Tell You, You Are My Life
Every Waking Moment, Not Second Goes By
Never Wished You As My Wife

You Have Blossomed, This Woman That You Are
Carrying Our Child Within Your Womb
Then Will Grow Up, To Look Beautiful In White
When She Will Marry, And There, Her Life Will Bloom

SOMETHING ABOUT YOU

There Was Something In Your Eyes

The Way You Looked At

Me

I Hoped This Connection Would

Never Be
Broken

Something About You

Something I Couldn't

Explain

A Sense Of Pleasance, An Entity
I Couldn't Help But
See

Imagined You Before Me, You Gestured

For No Words Be Needed Or

Spoken

Wanted You Near Me, Always

And Hoped You'd Always

Remain

There Was Something About You

How The Wind Caressed Your

Hair

As The Breeze, Blew Gently,

Like Something Out Of A Movie

Scene

I Pictured You By A Lake
Behind A Giant Oak
Tree

Leaves Fell, Collected At Your Feet
This, Nothing I Could
Compare
When Nothing Like This
Have I Ever
Seen
And Hope From This Dream,
I Would Never Be
Free
I Felt Sure, There's No One Else
You Entered My World, And I Ain't Leaving
Now
I'll Never Have This Chance Again,
A Chance To Be With
You
Though Through My Mind Of Lingering Doubts,
Must Believe That I
Can
I Will Travel The Distance To Get There
To Get To You
Somehow
And Together My Dear,
To Start A Life
Anew
Hand In Hand Forever
To Fulfill A Lifelong
Plan

TIME TRAVEL

Only Has It Ever Been Dreamed Of
To Travel Beyond The Here And Now
A Second Forward, A Second Past
Only Question Remains, Just How

Man Has Always Dreamt Of Travelling
Further And Beyond, Beyond The Stars And Galaxies
Books Written, Movies Made
These Fill Our Dreams With Fantasies

To Travel Faster Than The Speed Of Light,
In A Machine To Any Given Moment
Time Travel, All Made Possible In The Imagination
Given That The Speed Of Light, Can Be Broken

In Time Travel, Imagine A Journey Into Yesterday
Knowing All The Things That Will Unfold
To Meet, Perhaps A Different You
And Caution, What The Future Holds

Or A Day In The Future, A Day Beyond Today
Perhaps To A Time, You Wished You Had Not
What Will You Take Back With You?
Maybe The Lottery Numbers, To Win The Lot

Envisage, For A Moment, Time Travel,
Past, Presence And Future
At Your Very Hands, To Do As You Desired
To Go Back To See Who U Were…

Time Travel, Where Time And Space Act As One
Warp Speed, No Doubt Be Required
Like In Some Science Fiction Books
From HG Wells Novel, Inspired

Time Travel, Be It Fact Or Fiction, To Exceed
Expectations, To Make Fantasy Happen
To Enter Into Another State, The Fourth Dimension
And Only In Our Minds Can We Imagine

They Have Said, Back In Time
Space Travel Would Never Exist
And Going To The Moon, Was Unheard Of
And Too, Pictures Of Mars, They Dismissed

Time Travel, May, Yes, Seem Far Fetched
With This Ever-Increasing Desire To Dominate
Though Man Has Delved Into The Vast And Unknown
Time Travel Will Just Have To Wait

AS I LAY AND PONDER

As I Lay And Ponder Upon

This Sandy

Beach

Looking Up To The

Skies, And The Heaven,

Beyond

Putting Out My Hands

As If By Chance, Could

Reach

Nothing But Empty Space

If Life There Exists, Will It

Respond

Through The Billions Of Galaxies

Stars, Light Years

Away

As I Lay And Ponder, Watching

Shooting Stars

Collide

Atomic Explosion

Bursting With Lights In Colours

Array

This Splendour Of Nature

Taking It All In My

Stride

As The World Turns
My Eyes Closed, Visions
Of What Once
Seemed
From My Childhood Years
To The Man That I
Became
Is This The Past I'm Seeing?
Or Maybe I Just
Dreamed
The Life I Have Lived
Has Been Never In
Shame
With Endless Possibilities
Of Where My Life Could
Be
For The Future Upon Us, Has
Not Been
Set
In Time, Many Pathways
Shall We Open
Many Doors, With No
Key
Take The Road Leading Somewhere
Never Look Back, Never
Forget

My Fading Thoughts, Floating
Out To Sea, The
Ocean
As The Ripple Tides
Draws In To Kiss At My
Toes
A Sense Of Drifting, Like
My Body's Free, Set My Spirit In
Motion
Leaving Me To Explore The
Universe Or Whoever
Knows

BEFORE YOU GO

I Know Our Lives Ran A Separate
Path, Put Up With The Abuse You
Threw
I Know You've Found Another
Another, To Replace
Me
Someone With Whom, I
Could Not
Compete
A Fancy Car, A House By The Beach
On A Hill With A
View
Or Perhaps A Yacht, To Go
Sailing, In A Lake, On The
Sea
My Every Moment, Wanted You To
Stay, Now Shameful You Had
Cheat
So, Before You Go, Opening
The Door To
Leave
Is There Words To Say, Make
You Change Your
Mind

To Start Our Lives Over, To The
Way Things Used To
Be
Give Me Something To Restore
The Faith, And Something To
Believe
Wanting So Much To Be Together
To Restore A Love, So Once
Defined
I Cherished And Cared For You
Will He Be There Always, Will
He?
Do You Recall, I Took You Back?
Your Moods Ran Cold, Like A Stream Of Running
Water
The Many Times, Never Came Home
Was Worried
I'll
The Day, You Packed To Leave,
Left For Your
Mother
So Please, Before You Go
Consider Our Child, Our
Daughter

That Has Embraced Our Lives

With A Love, Now So

Filled

I Cannot Bear The Thought

Of You Leaving For

Another

So, Before You Go, Can You Please

Explain

SOMETIMES I WANNA QUIT

Sometimes I Wanna Quit When
Life Gets The Better of Us, Get Overwhelmed
Then A Voice Inside My Head Says Do It
When All I Ever Needed Was A Friend

But Then I Know I Can't,
Thinking, Who Will Care, If I Go Or Stay
Just Another Poor Soul To Meet His Maker
But Hope That In Your Name, They'll Pray

Was I Ever Good Enough?
What Was My Purpose, My Goal?
Were They Ever Achieved, When
At Last, My Body Departed My Soul

Yeah, Sometimes I Wanna Quit
But Who Will Be Left Behind
To Pick Up The Pieces When You're Gone
Anyone? Perhaps No One, You Will Find

There's A Nice View From Up Here
The Ocean Bellow Looks Rather Clear
It Shouldn't Take Long, A Short Moment
But Suddenly, That Dreaded Feeling Of Fear

The Body Starts To Tremble
The Wind Builds Up, Struggling To Hold On
It Must Be One Hundred Metres Below
Only A Minute, Then You're Gone

The Eyes Make Focus Towards
The Crashing Waves Upon The Rocks, Jagged
Sight Growing Dim, Blurred
And Trying To Control My Trembling Hand

From Up Here, The Lighthouse Signals
Out To Sea, Alerting Ill Fated Seamen,
The Crew Upon A Trawler
Perhaps Facing Their Inner Demons

Then Suddenly, Like A Movie On Fast Forward
I'm Left Alone, Still Standing Upon This Height
Forgetting The Reason I'm Here In The First Place
Sometimes I Wanna Quit, Or, For My Life I Will Fight

You Have Failed Yourself, Failed In Life
An Echo Drilling Inside My Brain
What Reasons Have I To Continue?
There's Nothing Else To Gain

Sometimes, You Wanna Quit
Because It's Easier To Give In
Then To Deal With Life's Problems
That Can Stem From Within

MONEY CAN'T BUY…

All His Life He Worked
To Live A Life Of Luxury
To Buy His Wife Things From
The Best China, To The Finest Cutlery

To Shower His Family With Things
As A Kid, He Never Had
Perhaps A Fancy House, A Car
Or A Supporting Dad

Waiting For The Numbers To Drop In
The Lottery Draw, That May Fulfil His Dreams
Wouldn't Have To Work Again
Spoil His Wife And Kids With All Their Needs

Frustration Grows, Filled With Disappointment
Eyes Grow With Rage, Another Failed Attempt
"Honey! Can We Go To The Beach Now?"
"Not Now', With Ire And Contempt

"I Didn't Win," "But You Promised The Kids"
"I'm Not In The Mood"
"Honey! Money Can't Buy You Happiness
"What We Need Is Love And Food"

"You Don't Understand,
I Wanted To Buy You Things To Have The Best
Get Away From This Hellhole
And Give Up Work, There, I'm Always Stressed

"To Start A New Life, A House By The Beach"
Best Colleges For Our Sons
"I Wanted To Spoil You, With
A Five Bedroom House, With The Money We Won

Honey! I Have All I Need,
I Am Happy As You Are, Rich Or Poor
I Married You In Sickness And In Health
I Love You, For Whatever You Choose

Money Can't Buy Love, Or Inner Peace
Patience And A Mutual Respect
It Cannot Buy The Time You Give Us
Can Only Buy You Things And Objects

As He Held His Head Down In Shame
"Daddy! This Is A Drawing I Made, Us, At The Beach
"That's Me, Mummy, Baby Joel And You
And The Balloon, He Was Trying To Reach

"Thank You Sweetie! That's Really Awesome
His Mind Wondered, And Without Delay
"OK! Who Wants To Go To The Beach?"
"I Do Daddy, Can We Stay The Day"

Laughing "We Will See"
"Darling! I'm Sorry If I Seemed A Little Foolish"
Can You Ever Forgive Me?
"There's Nothing To Forgive, But As You Wish

"You Are Right Sweetheart"
Money Can't Buy Us Happiness
We Have Each Other, That's What Counts
And The Love, That Will Carry Us.

"I'll Promise To Make Things Right
Work Hard And Put More Hours
So, You'll Never Be Without
And Everything Will Be Ours

NATURES GIFT

The Sun Rises As The Dusk Fades
Across The Land, Across The Fields
Critters Scurry In Search Of Food
As Farmers Harvest The Crop To Yield

Nature's Gift With Its Earthly Splendour
A Calf – Newborn Sees Its First Day
First Steps With Trembling Paces
Falls To The Turf, And There It Stays

The Wind Sails, The Calf, No Notice It Takes
As Flowers Bloom In A Perpetual Motion
Into The Gentle Breeze, It Spreads It Sweetly Scents
Nature's Gifts Caresses The Land With Devotion

At A Distance, Swirling Clouds
A Drenching Downpour, Soon To Become
When Heavens Open Up In A Thunderous Rage
Will Stop At Nothing Whence It Will Come

The Skies Clear, Looking To The Grandeur
Of My Country Side, Far As The Eye Can See
Cascading Waterfalls, Trickling On The Eroded Hills
But I Know, From Nature's Gift I Shan't Be Set Free

Like A Photograph, My Mind Captures
This God Given Land, That Many Have Trodden
This, My Home, My West Virginia
Over- Shadowed, That Time Has Long Forgotten

Where The Mountains Meet The Sky
And Snow-Capped Ridges Refract The Light
My Eyes, To This Beauty, I Admire
There's Nothing On Earth, With Such Delight

Upon Crystal Lakes, Swans, Like Maidens Dance,
Cygnets, Trailing Slowly Behind
Through The Ripples
With Elegance, Gracefully They Glide

Guarding Their Nest From Would Be Predators,
Necks Entwined To A Heart Shape Pose
Circling, To Their Ritual Love Song
Nature's Gifts Upon That Lake, Flows

As The Ebb Tides Flows In, Flows Out
Night Falls Again, The Moon, Across The Sky Sweeps
Over My Paradise Sphere
When The World Falls Silently To Sleep

And When It Awakens, A New Day Will Dawn
Then Our Spirits Will Again Lift
And In Awe We Will Marvel
At The Sights Of Nature's Gift

MY SON

No Son Wants To Hear From His Father
"You'll Never Mount To Anything My Boy
Go Out And Make Something Of Your Life
Find A Girl For You To Enjoy"

I Was His Disappointment Child
An Outcast By Society
Could Never Look Me In The Eyes
Which Then Brought About My Anxiety

You See, I Was Different From All The Other Boys
Some Played With Cars
Getting Their Hands Dirty In The Mud
Well, Me, I Went Chasing Stars

I Lived In A World Of Make Believe
Of Unicorns And Fairies
They Do Exist You Know
Was Never One, For Chasing Glories

I Cried Often, No One Knew Why
My Mother, Well The Bottle Being In Control
My Father, Wasn't A Father Figure
So Never Played The Role

I Was To Blame, For Whatever Did Happen
My Son, Why Can't You Do Anything Right
"But Dad, It Wasn't Me"
Just Accused Me Out Of Spite

I Ran Away From Life And Responsibilities
Lived To Everyone's Expectations
And Never My Own
Or For That Matter My Obligations

My Son, Why Can't You Be Like Your Brother
With A Wife And A Family
With Another On The Way
Living His Life Happily

But Dad, I Am Not Him
Or Ever Will Be
Accept Me As I Am, Who I Am
I Hope One Day You Will Wake And See

"I Knew The Day You Were Born
That You Were Very Different
Told Your Mum, She Never Listened
Why Can't You Live, As Life Was Meant?"

He Tried To Change How I Looked
Said I Was Never Good Enough
"You Have No Respect For Yourself, This Family
You Are Weak, Never Will Be Tough

The Years Have Slowly Diminished
My Father Is Aging, My Mother Has Passed
Still To This Day, Not Even A Hug, A Kiss
In His Eyes, I'm Still That Outcast

He Died Just Yesterday Gone
But With The Words He Uttered From His Lips
In His Death Bed, My Son I Love You
Just Before He Slipped

Into The Great Divide, Where
Souls, Meet Their Holiest Divine
As They Follow The Stairwell In The Sky
As Life, Was So Defined

NEVER SAY NEVER

Never Say Never My Mother
Used To Preach
She'd Say Son, Whatever You Want
You Can Have You Can Reach

She Went On To Say
When You Stumble And Fall
Get Back Up
But As Long As You Gave It Your All

Try Never To Surrender
And Cling On To Life
In The Face Of Adversity
Trouble And Strife

Never Say Never, My Child
Her Arms Around Me Tightly
The Spirit Conquers The Highest Mountain
And The Light, Will Shine Upon You, Brightly

You Will March With A Head Held High
And A Victory Song Is What We'll Sing
Never Looking Back
But Look Forward, To What The Future Brings

When You Sail Upon The Sea Of Despair
And The Clashing Waves Come Spiralling,
The Fear Of Doubt, Will Pierce Your Heart
But I Know Your Bravery'll Come Hurling

Those Stormy Nights Cannot Hold You
And Though The Roads Ahead Stretches Wide
With Every Bend, A New Beginning
So, Take Hold, The Steering Wheel, And Ride

Unleash The Fury, I Know You Possess
As The Fighter That's Inside Of You
And Never Lose Sight
Of The Hero, You Once Were And Knew

Never Say Never
To The Journey, That's An Upward Climb
Many Dreams Are Lost, Many Are Gained
But It's Only Just A Matter Of Time

The Goal Is Right In Front
See It, Grasp, And Take A Hold
But Never Say Never
For It Is Worth The Weight In Gold

Like A Phoenix Through The Flames
May You Rise Above The Perilous Wrecks
Never Say Never, When Breath
Is Within You To Prepare What Follows Next

You Never Thought That You Could Fly
Or Take A Leap Of Faith
Against All Odds, You Persevered And
Triumphed, When Doubt Came Face To Face

You Found The Strength Within
Rose Higher To The Sky
There Was No Turning Back
Never Knew, Till That Day You Tried

Never Say Never
Till The Day You Breathe Your Last
Look Back, And Know You Gave It Your All
If God Should One Day Ask

There Is No Gain Without Pain
So Much That It Would Hurt
So Never Say Never
Let The Life Within, From You, Burst

When The Paths Of Life
Lead You Astray
And Potholes, Many To Encounter,
Never Are They Even, Or Ever To Go Away

So, Face Up To Your Fears
There Is No Going Back
A Beam Of Light To Show And Guide You
To Set Your Life On Track

A BIRTHDAY WISH

A Birthday Wish From Across The Miles
To Letting You, Someone Does Care
We've Only Just Briefly Met
If Ever In Need, Hon, I'll Be There

To Lend A Crying Shoulder
To Make You Laugh And Smile
On Your 49th Birthday
What Can I Offer, Perhaps To Stay Awhile?

I May Not Be There In Body
But In My Spirit, There Ill Dwell
To Be Your Guardian Angel
This, To You I'll Tell

Michelle, You're More Than A Friend
I Have Come To Realise
At Times, Feeling Wanting More
Opened To You, And Hon, This, I Tell No Lies

I've Been There Through Your Ups And Downs
The Happy And The Sad Times
Shared In The Laughter
And In My Verses And Rhymes

Your Tipsy Moments Lol, And Were Many
But You Always Came To Shine
The Smiles, They Were Infectious
I Guess, It's How You Were Designed

Just A Birthday Wish
To Hope That This Poem Finds You Well
On Your Birthday, December 17th
What More Can I Tell

Don't Ever Give Up On Your Dreams
They Make You Who You Are
You May Not Get There
But You'll Always Be, A Shining Star

Your 49th Birthday Wish
And Hon, That's A Lotta Candles
Be Sure To Blow Each Out
And Mind To Watch, Those Love Handles

Which I, Incidentally Love
In Fact, Every Piece Of Your Being
Yes, Your Mind Too, Lol
Be Sure, To Lay That Upon Me

Just To See You Smile
Nothing More, Will I Ask
A Safe And Happy Birthday
Should Not Be A Mean Task
HAPPY 49TH HON
ALL THE VERY BEST.

LOVE FROM HENRY
YOUR TIKTOK AUSTRALIAN FRIEND

WHAT THE DEAF MAN HEARD

He Wasn't Able To Hear Voices Or Sounds
Couldn't Utter Words
The World Of Silence Was His Only Friend
Often Longed To Hear The Twitter Of Birds

Never Knew Sounds Existed
Quiet Is What The Deaf Man Heard
Though He Could Not Convey Speech,
Words In The Air, Is What He Preferred

He Heard With His Eyes, And
Spoke Through His Fingers
Rhythmic Motions Gestured In Fluency
To Anyone That Watched, Beauty Lingers

Motion Upon Motion, His Fingers Twirled
Like A Mime Artist, His Imagery World's, A Reality
What The Deaf Man Heard, We Don't Know
But Ask Him To Sign An Image, Of Fiction Or Fantasy

The World Of Emptiness, All He's Ever Known
Never To Hear A Dog, In The Alley Street Barking
The Sounds From A Baby Crying He Couldn't Hear
Never The Sounds Of People's Natter, When Idle Talking

What The Deaf Man Heard, Pictures In The Air
Swirling, Was Like Music To His Eyes
They Motioned In Flowing Rhymes
Like A Melody Set To Gestural Signs

Never To Hear The Radio's Tunes And Tones
Or Orchestra Bands, And Their Sound
He Was Blessed With The Gift Of Sign
Born Of No Hearing, So Profound

People Pass By, Smile And Wave Hello
Sign "Good-Bye" As They Leave
Watching, With A Smile Upon His Face
To His Amazed Eyes, Cannot Quite Believe

He Reads Lips Without Hesitations Or Flaws
He Lives In The Silence, That's His Deaf World
Reading Body Language, He's Aptly Suited
Do You Know What The Deaf Man Heard?

IF ONLY

Life Ends Slowly As It
Begins, Passes Before Our Very
Eyes
We Take For Granted The
Air We Breathe, Then It's Too
Late
We Will Perish From This
Earth, And Everything That's Ours
Dies
We May Die Before Time
And Look Back With
Regrets, Entering Pearly
Gates
If Only I Did That, Accomplished
More Than I
Did
My Life Laid Waste Gave
Into My
Fears
Had Many Ambitions,
I Remember, Growing Up As A
Kid
My Life Took A Turn
Venturing Into My Adult
Years

How I Truly Felt About
You, I Could Not
Admit
If Only The Courage
Within Had
Grown
I Guess At That Time
My Affection To Anyone,
I Did Not
Commit
You Cared For Me, This
Much I Know, But Love
Was Never Carved In
Stone
If Only I Stood Up For
Myself When Pushed The
Many Times, I
Fell
Bullied And Abused Made
Feel Less Of A
Man
And To Those Around
Me, None I Couldn't
Tell

When Problems I Faced
Between The Eyes, Thought
To Myself, "Solve This I
Can"
Never Had Directions, No
Maps To Guide
Through
If Only I'd Followed My
Desires The Passions In My
Life
Made Something Special,
Set Goals I Had To
Pursue
To Fight Off Adversity
To Fight Off Life's Bitter
Strife…
If Only We Had Gotten
Together, Instead- The Constant
Fights
Life's Moments Are Short
Never Knowing If These Be Our
Last
Stayed Up Till The Morning
Thinking If We'll Ever
Reunite

Treasure Those Endearing
Moments, If Ever They Be Our
Past
Time Speeds Up, Waits
For No Man, And They
Say
Each Moment We Inhale
A Second Goes
By
If Time Stood Still, I'd Watch
The World Whirl Around
I'd Never Leave
Today
So Many Question That
I Would Ask, But Never Ask
Why
My Life, Like A Picture
In A Movie
Scene
Take After Take, Memorizing
Those Every
Lines
If Only It Was Real. I Wouldn't
Hide Like The Actors On The
Screen

No Instructions To Help
Me, No Rules To Follow
Only The Remnants Of Washed Out
Signs
My Family Through The
Years, I Have Failed To
See
If Only I Had Rang Them
Seen How They
Were
My Children Now In
Their Adult Prime. Would
They Even Know
Me
Or My Wife, Went Our
Separate Way, Would I Now Know
Her
At Times, My Life Seen Often
Sheltered, No
Risks
Missing Out On What Might
Have Been A
Memory
But Flowing Emotions Of
A Little Boy- Me, When I Was But
Six

If I Died Tomorrow Would
The World Recall Or
Remember Me.
If Only I Had Lived In
This Presence, In The Here And
Now
I Would See The World
As It Is, These Moments, This
Day
I Would Accept My
Being, Without Wondering
Of Why Or
How
Just To Be Living, And That
I'm Here To Live. To
Stay
If Only I Had Taken More
Chances, Or Worried, So
Much
If I Enjoyed The Ride Of My
Life, I'd Be Filled With
Wisdom
And My Sanity I'd Miss If
Only I had Kept In
Touch

But Life Ain't That Easy

As Light Shines Through A

Prism

Reaching Decisions, Many

I Did Not

Make

Choices, Confusions

Against A

Belief

Bred Resentment From

People, Friends Who Were

Fake

And Bitterness Only Lead

To Heartache And

Grief

If Only

DON'T GIVE UP

It Is Said That We Come

To This Earth With
Nothing

And Truly At Times, Life

Deals Us A Hand We Cannot

Use

Don't Give Up When You Fall,

Rise, Become Someone, Achieve
Something

When Opportunities Knock,

Take With Both Hands, And Never

Refuse

The Roads We Travel May

Never Lead To Where We Wanna

Go

No Maps To Guide Us

No Arrows

Pointing

Which Direction? Many Times

We'll Never Really

Know

And Left Stranded On

A Corner, Just

Waiting

Learning To Walk At Just
Months Of
Age

He Falls And Cries, But
Gets Up To Try Once
Again
Mummy's Loves You,
Watching His Every
Stage
Don't Give Up Dear! I Know
How Much It's Hurting
And You're In
Pain
When We Give Up, We
Fail, We
Fall
Learning To Get Up, Finding
The Courage, Trying Once
More
Create Yourself, Be That
Person Who Stands Above
All
Don't Give Up, Believe
What You Stand
For

When One Door Closes Another Shall Open
Life Goes On
Taste The Knowledge We Have Learnt

A WOMAN'S SCENT

In Some Stranded Bar Of Town
Her Beauty, Unveiled Before Me
Caressing Her Glass With A Two Finger Stroke
Her Gestures, Established, I Was Quick To See

Her Fragrance Filled The Air
With Her Alluring Perfume
Eyes On Her
When She Entered The Room

From Across The Room, She
Stood There, Waiting To Be Seen
One Glance At Her, My Imagination
Played, Like In Some Movie Scene

Touching Her Lips, I Was In A Daze
Her Woman's Scent Lingered
Heads Did Turn, And Across
My Body, Hairs Stood On End, Skin Tingled

Her Cheeks, Like A Rosy Blossom, Bloomed
Beauty Before My Eyes Would Excite
Was She Out Of My Reach?
But In My Heart, I Felt She Was Just Right

Dreamt Of Moments Just To Be With Her
But Only In My Dreams Do I See
Even There, I'd Smell That Woman's Scent
No Rose, As Fragile As She

One On One, Our Eyes Gazed
Took Her Hand Into Mine
Only A Smile Did We Share
That Never A Painting Could Ever Define

Her Moves Captivating, Her Shapely Figure
With Her, I Wanted To Be Alone
Make Her Special, Make Her Mine
How Could I Make My Feelings Known?

Her Feminine Grace
Her Infectious Charm
Beauty, Enticing In My Presence
My Body, Quivered Yet So Calm

So Awe Inspiring
My Eyes Never Set Upon Such Bliss
No Woman, So Ever Filled With Essence
This Opportunity, I Shan't Ever Miss

And In My Mind, I Approached Her
Not Holding Back, No Hesitation
Her Woman's Scent
Calmed My Nervy Situation

I Found The Courage To Say "Hi"
Smiling Back She Said "Hello"
Here's My Chance I Thought
As Her Eyes Glisten, Into A Radiant Glow

Her Woman's Scent,
An Aroma Sweetly Breathing
Her Body, I Longed To Hold
And From Her, I Would Not Be Leaving

Like A Teenager On Heat
My Pheromones Escalated
Palms Sweating Profusely
Anxiety On High, Elevated

Nothing Could Have Prepared Me
For What Happened Next
A Kiss She Blew For Me To Catch
And Like Some Fairytale Became Hexed

I Was Under Her Spell
Mesmerized, Nothing I Wouldn't Do For Her
A Tightrope I Would Walk Upon
Walk On Burning Flames Of Ember

I Will Adore Her Make Feel Special
Just To Breathe In, Her Woman's Scent
And If I Should Lose Her
I Would Understand, What Without Her Meant

YOU'LL NEVER KNOW

I Sit And Marvel The Life I Have Lived
Watching Birds Flying The Open Skies
Dogs In The Back Scene Barking
Kids Frolicking, Mothers Nursing Her Baby's Cries

I Ponder At Life, And What It
Means To Lose A Child, If Never A Parent
Or To See Them Growing
From Birth Till Adolescent

Life Always Seems
To Slap Us On The Face
To Awaken Us, If We May Lag Behind
To Continue Our Journey In This Human Race

So Much, I've Not Yet Lived
A Bucket List, Not Yet Started
Having No Time, Is A Bad Excuse
Seemed Always Tired And Jaded

You'll Never Know, The Times I've Tried
To Fulfill My Dreams
But Always Tomorrow I Think,
Tomorrow Never Comes, So It Seems

I'm Not Getting Any Younger
I Keep Myself Reminded
When A Voice Inside Me, Urging Me
Don't Look Back And From The Truth, Be Blinded

You'll Never Know What
Thoughts That I Hide,
Or The Waves Of Uncertainty
I Keep Swept Aside

The Words I Have Been Meaning To Say
Or Dreams And Aspiration, I've Never Told
But Silently The Tears That I Weep
Burst Out, Uncontrolled

You'll Never Know,
Of The Nights That I Couldn't Sleep
Thinking About You
Leaving Me Scarred Within My Heart, Deep

Or The Hope That I Had Lost
Bitter, As The Cold Winter's Chills
Left Me Frightened With Despair
And My Body, With A Fear That Over Spills

You'll Never Know, What Lies
Hidden In My Saddened Heart
Nor Will You Ever Grasp The Extent Of Me
Feeling, We Are Drifting Apart

Will You Ever Know The Times
That I've Missed You
When You Weren't Around
Rang Your Phone, Honey If Only You Knew

You Always Seemed Out, Left You Messages
That You Cared Less To Reply
Wanting To Say How I Missed You
But All I Could Do, Was Try

I Wanted To Make Each Day
A Lasting Moment
No Regrets, Just You And I Together
On A Cruise Enjoying The Time We've Spent

You'll Never Know The Passion Inside Of Me
Till We Have Embraced And Kissed
How I Have Longed For Your Presence
And When Not There, I Have Missed

Take A Chance, Dare To Be Different
Life Is Not A Win Or A Losing Game
Let Us Go As One
And Rekindle Our Love's Burning Flame

You'll Never Know
When Any Breath You Take, Be Your Last
Or If You May Never To Awaken
We Take For Granted, Life, Before You Know, It's Passed

Keep Your Dreams In Sight
We Don't Know What The Future Holds
Or If At All There Will Be One
What Lies Ahead, Will Surely Unfold

Will Anyone Remember You
When You Are Dead And Gone
I Guess You'll Never Know
Buried In The Grave, Going To The Beyond

One Thing Certain
You Will Never Know
What Lies Beyond This Sphere?
Who'll Greet You, If In Heaven Or Below

STOLEN LOVE

You Said You'd Take Care Of My Heart

But Instead, You Stole My

Love

What Was Once Ours, You

Squandered On

Another

My Trust You Abused, Gone,

Taken For Granted, Amidst Our Cherished

Dreams

All My Life, I've Searched For You

Someone To Be A Part

Of

And To Be With Her, Think Of

Her, Id Much Not

Rather

When You Said You Loved Me

And All That I Meant To You

Your Love, Never As It

Seemed

Never Wanted Much

To Have A Life, A Family,

Children Of Our

Own

You Said Some Day,
This Day Never
Happened

Was I Not Pretty Enough?
That You Sought Else
Where
The Love We Once Shared
Crumbled When It Turned To
Stone
After Years Of Devotions
Emotionally Paralysed,
Never Could've
Imagined
Your Stolen Love, Emptied
My Heart, And Never Will I
Care
A Friend, I Once Called Mine
But Stole My Love For An Image More
Curved
What You Gave, Just Empty Promises
When You Promised Me The
World
I Didn't Mind Your Lies
But You Broke My Heart Along The
Way
I Forgave You Multitude Times
Much More Than You
Deserved

My Mind Lost In Confusion
When In Turmoil, It Was Me You
Hurled
You Were The Light To Guide Me
Now Only A Shadow Shall
Stay
You Made Excuses
I Have Nothing Left For You
Just Nothing Left At
All
Wish I Knew Where To Find You Again
But Our Paths, Broken, Beyond
Repair
Your Stolen Love, Etched
Inside Deep
Inside
The Life You've Stolen,
The Love You Maimed, Now Hidden
Barricaded By An Invisible
Wall
No More Tears To Cry
My Life In Abandonment,
Fallen Into
Despair
Never Will You Steal My Love
No More Will I Hurt, However Ways You
Try

STOLEN SILENCE

Silence All Around,
A Clear Sky With Stars Speckled
The Moon Over The Shores
Waves Shimmered Then Slowly Settled

The Stillness Taken Away
Only The Quiet Sounds Of Nature
Nearby Trees, Leaves Rustling
Makes Ways, A Majestic Feature

The Rivers And Lakes, Trickling From Mountain Tops
Running Water Gushes, A Photo Scene
In Slow Animated Motion
Nature In Its Purity, Serene

While The World Begins To Sleep,
Outside, Myriads Of Bats Take To Flight
With Echoing Clicks And Chirps
What Was Once Peaceful, Now Deafens The Night

Ear Drums Throbbing, Beating
Engulfed, By The Heightened Pitch
No One Dares Approaches Near, Or
Come Out Alive, Without A Hitch

With The Intensity, Growing Louder,
My Thoughts, If By Now I Have Any
Have Succumbed To Their Absence
Where Before There Were Many

In The Stolen Silence, Struggling
To Hear Above The Raucous Sounds
The Pitched Intense, Would
Suddenly Disappear All Around

Nocturnal Critters Scurry On By
Outside My Window, Under Dimmed Light
They Would Disturb The Peace
When Suddenly, Vanish Out Of Sight

Amidst The Stolen Silence, Was
Robbed Of My Unclouded Serenity
And The Peaceful Calmness, Which
Blurred My Clarity

Was Woken From My Slumber
In A Neighbourhood Of Screeching Cars
The Sirens Came Blaring
Gunshots Fired, Now A Man Behind Bars

A Woman Lay Screaming
In Her Pool Of Blood, Spouting
When No One Came Near
No Heed They Took To Her Shouting

In That Instance Of The Stolen Silence
Not A Word Be Heard
No Crowd Had Ever Gathered
Nor sympathy had ever occurred

NEVER GIVE UP ON US

We Went To Bed In Silence
Over Harsh Things We Needn't Have Said
I Know We Didn't Mean Them
We Should've Made Up Instead

If I Could Tell You My Feelings
Please Never Give Up On Us
Time Has The Means Of Mending
The Heart, If Only, In Each Other-Trust

Even If The World Stopped Turning
Even If Our Paths Went A Separate Way
Never Give Up On Us
Or Be Tempted To Turn Me Away

I Will Forever Be There,
To Pick You Up And Carry You Through
I Will Be The Light To Guide Us
I'd Want You, In My Arms, You'll Fall Into

Never Thought, I'll Ever Love You
As Much As I Do Right Now
Though Words Have Come Between Us
We Can Make This Work, If You Allow

Never Give Up On Us
On What We Had, Do Have And Will
Don't Shut Me Out Now
Coz, I Am Loving You Still

I Would Feel Empty, My Heart Would Die
You Are The Air That I Breathe
My Blood, Through My Veins That Flows
You Are, What Makes My Life Complete

Never Give Up On Us, So Much I Wanna Do
And Tonight, We Only Have Each Other
We Can't Take That Away, When
We Can Take This Much Further

I Need You To Know This, You're My
Knight In Shining Armour
Fight For Me, As I Would For You
I Can Be Your Everything And Far More

If You Leave Us, What Do We Have
Nothing But Empty Dreams, No More Promises
No Purpose To Live, No Nothing At All
Lose All We Had, All Our Accomplishes

So Much That We Can Share,
Hand In Hand, Along The Beach
The Sun As It Sets
Heights, We Have Not Yet Reached

Never Give Up On Us
Times, I Know Will Get Tough
Aren't We Worth Enough, To Take A Chance
Though the paths ahead May Be Rough

WAKE ME FROM THIS SLEEP

I Was Dreaming Of You
To Bed, Late Last
Night
Wake Me From This Sleep
And Hoping You Are
Real
To Touch You, Feel You
That Everything Bout You Is
True
I Can't Go On At The Thought
Of Losing This
Fight
Hold Me, Holding You, To
Know How You
Feel
Together, Forever And
That You Love Me
Too
Wake Me From This Sleep
From A World, Of Make
Believe
Just Fragmented Thoughts
What Is Real, What Is
Not
At Times, Drifting Further
From The Truth, From
Reality

When My Eyes Will Open
To Be By Your Side, And Will Never
Leave
To Acknowledge Your Goodness
And Appreciate, What I've
Got
Wake Me From This Sleep
I Know I've Heard You
Calling
My Name, In The Whispering Voice
Of A Gentle
Breeze
Your Arms Stretched Out
Running To You, Seems So Far
Away
The Sun Is Rising, Up Ahead
Will Soon Be
Morning
I Cannot Stand, This Trance
Like State, This World Of Illusion
That Reality Cannot
Seize
Must Get To You, My Darling
Somehow, In Some Possible
Way
Just Please Please Wake Me
From This Mindless, State Of
Sleep

CHASING THE DREAMS

I Wasn't Like Any Other Boys Growing Up
Teased And Chased, They Called Me Names
From A Poor Family
Never Included In The Fun And Games

They Said, I Would Never Amount To Anything
That I'd Fail In The Things I Tried
I Couldn't Run. I Couldn't See
Somehow Knew I'd Succeed, If I Applied

An Old Piano That Sat In The Back
One That Was Never Used
It Was By Accident, I Stumbled Upon It
For Hours, This Kept Me Amused

Tinkling At The Ivories, Just Noise
Filling The Air, With Random Sounds
I Played That Thing, All Day And Night
My Talent I Thought I Might Have Found

Thinking This Was It,
Mother, Stood Behind, Unbeknown To Me
Trusted, I Was Chasing My Dream
Too Young To Realise, But This She Would See

A Phone Call She Had Made
Enrolled Me In One On One Lessons,
A Teacher Of Music, He Came To Our House
Noted I Was Gifted With An Essence

As Time Went On, That Old Grand
Became A Friend And Music Filled The Air
Began Writing Notes, Eventually
Songs, I Wrote That Year

Chasing The Dreams, When Music Was My Passion
When No-One Believed, Mother Was There
With Words Of Encouragement
I Knew She Did Care

I Had Faith In Myself, I Had No Regrets
When People Are Hurtful, At Times, Unkind
Go Follow Your Dreams, And If You
Don't Give In, It's Success You Will Find

Don't Live In The Past, I Told Myself
There's So Much I Had To Achieve
When You Are Chasing Your Dreams
In Yourself You Have To Believe

I Left My Past Behind, Cared Less
What Anyone Had Said
They Made Me Find My Talent
Chose To Rise Above It All, Instead

To This Day I Still Remember
Humiliation Growing Up, Then A Kid
I Found A Dream To Chase
Not All Do Come True, I Just Know, That Mine Did

I DON'T KNOW

How Do I Know If I Am In Love?
I Really Have No Idea,
I Just Don't Know
I Think Of Her Often, It Seems To Appear

But I Still Don't Know If I Am
It Started As Just A Friendship
We'd Joke Around, Going Places
Without Warning, I'm Doing Backflips

I Was Just Being Silly I Guess
Or Maybe I Was Showing Off
Yeah, I Suppose She Was A Special Girl
The Way She Offered Water, As I Began To Cough

Standing Beside Her
My Hands, No Reason, Become Sweaty
Trying To Speak, Tongue Tied
Thoughts Came Gushing "How Lovely, How Pretty

For The First Time, Lost For Words
Did Not Turn Out Right
My Heart Started To Beat Faster
Having Her With Me, Was Such A Delight

Like No Other, I Have Felt This
No Other, I'd Spend So Much Of My Time
Perhaps Cupid's Love Arrows Had Landed
Am I Thinking Too Far Ahead, Hearing Bells Chime?

It Was To Early To Tell,
To Even Contemplate That M Word
Butterflies In Your Stomach
A Sure Sign I Am, So I've Heard

Wanting To Hold Her Palms
Should I, Shouldn't, Mine Were Wet
The Attraction Was Building Up
Just Like In Romeo And Juliet

Is This Love, I Really Don't Know?
Wanted To Ask Her Out, Became Speechless
My Words, Came Stuttered
And The Night, Sleepless

"Good Morning Honey"
First Message Of The Day, To Her
"What Did I Just Say" I Couldn't Believe
"Great! Where To From Here"?

"That's It I Have To Ask Her Out"
Thinking I'll See Her Again Sometime Later
But For Now, Time For A Cold Shower
Before, Tonight I Would Date Her

Put On My Best Cologne
Best Suit And Attire, Surely Will Impress
Yeah! I Know It's Only MacDonald's
But At Sixteen, It's A Meal, Nevertheless

Is This Love Or Lust That I'm Feeling
I Don't Know, But Feels Good
A Hunger For Her Affection Texting Her "Hi Julie"
"Wanna Go Out To Eat Later", I Hope You Would"

"Sure! Where To?"
How About McDonalds, "Sorry, I'm A Vegetarian"
"That's Ok, We Can Eat Healthy"
"Thanks," "I Know This Place, It's Hungarian"

"Yep! Sounds Great, What Time?"
How About In Half An Hour?
"Ok I'll Get Ready, Won't Take Long

"Is This The Real Thing, I Don't Know
Right Now, My Hormones Are In Disarray
A Chemical Build Up, I Cannot Control
I've Never Felt This Way

Music Beating In My Heart
A Sense Of Euphoria, Over Joy
The Nerves Haven't Set In Just Yet
I Will See Her Soon, My Charm, I Will Employ

Flowers In My Hand, Ready To Give
"Hi, How Are Ya!"! These Are For You
"Aww! You Shouldn't Have, But Thanks"
Sexual Desires, Mounting, Upon Me, Grew

A Peck On The Cheek, She Went Red
"Hope That Was Ok, You Didn't Mind"
No! That Was Fine, You're So Sweet
There, Before Me, Beauty So Defined

Is This Love, I Don't Know, Or Maybe I Do
She's The One I Think Of Every Morning, Every Night
In The Times I Am Alone, Or When I'm Not
If It Feels Good, It Must Be Right

HIDING BEHIND THE PAST

Your Past Shaded In Gloom
A Prisoner Of Your Own
Devise
A Life You Spent In Solitude
No One Came Near Or
Allowed
You Confined Yourself, Barricaded
From The
World
What's It Like, Hiding Deceit
Behind The
Lies
Was Your Head In Confusion
In Disarray, When Immersed In The
Clouds
An Outcast, Banished From
Society, It Was You, They
Hurled
A World Of Fiction, Living
On The Lies, You Hide
Behind
A Mask You Used To
Masquerade The
Truth

Falling To Deception, Your
Mind Blurred From
Reality
No Sight To See The Truth
Your World's A Prison Cell, To Which
You Became
Confined
You Tried Hiding Behind The Past
Became Enslaved, To Your
Youth
Your Life Was One, Never Free
Perhaps A Story Book
Fantasy
Depicted With Illusions Like A
Kaleidoscope Of
Emotions
Revolving, Endless Like Multitudes
Of Colours, The Blues And Reds In
Technicolour
Hiding Behind The Past
What Was Real, What Was
Not
Could You Ever Look In The Mirror
And Of Life, Have Any
Notions

The Family That Raised You,
Your Mother, Did Ever You Love
Her?
Perhaps All Is Lost
No Memories To Share
Remembering, Maybe You Just
Cannot

THIS BATTLE I MUST FIGHT

This Battle I Must Fight
Every Morning Getting Out Of Bed
Not Knowing What Was Instilled Upon Me
What Lay Before Me, Ahead

I Head For The Shower
To The Warm Water, Soothing And Calm
With Soap To Lather My Body
And Lotion Upon My Cupped Palm

Raising My Arm To Administer A Self-Test
As Every Woman Should
In And Around My Fleshy Tissue Of My Breast
Examining As Much As I Could

Something Round
That Aroused My Suspicion
So, Triple Zero I Quickly Rang
To Get Perhaps, A Second Opinion

"Hello, Emergency, How Can I Help You"
"Hi, I'd Like To Speak With Someone Re A Lump I Found"
"A Lump In Your Breast Ma'am"
"Yes" "We'll Need To Do An Ultra-Sound"

So, To The Hospital I Raced
Test Upon Test, Prodded And Poked
With A Sense Of Privacy Invasion
Not What I Wanted, Or Had Hoped

They Were Doctors After All, I Thought
It Was Confirmed What I Had Expected
"Can You Come Back Tomorrow, Further Tests
So, I Arrived Next Day, As Was Directed

As Tears From My Eyes Ran,
Shouting, This Cannot Be Real
Begging To The Doctor, Please Say This Isn't So
But Nothing More, He Would Reveal

"I'm Afraid We're Going To Administer
Chemo And Radiation Just To Be Certain"
It Was This Battle I Came To Fight
With No Choices, To Be Given

Losing My Hair, This I Realized
When Plagued With This Crippling Disease
All The While Thinking
Fighting For My Life, And Any Hope, I Can Seize

My Body Seems Never My Own
In A Mirror, Seeing Myself, Not As Was Designed
Clumps Of Hair Now Came Falling
I Was Changing, My Spirit Within, Had Declined

I Was Prepared For The Worst
Was This The Fate I Was Not Looking Forward To
My Life, Has Not Yet Been Lived
Wanting To Tackle Whatever Life Threw

Will I Lose Who I Am, Or Who I Was Born To Be
If My Womanhood Went Under The Knife
I Wanted To Cry, Emotions, Over Flow
This, Was No Way To End A Life

Voices In My Head, "Stay Positive
I Will Survive This"
I Will Not Lay Down, Nor Will I Plea
Stay Firm Till The End, If The Life In Me, Permits

I Will Not Bow Down In Defeat
As My Sister, Who Had Perished Before,
Who Remained Strong Till The Very End
With The Bravery In Their Hearts, They Wore

They May Have Fallen Victims
But With Pride They Lifted Their Heads
And With Courage On Their Sleeves
Walked Together As Friends

We'll Celebrate Pink Ribbon Day
With Dignity And Courage
And Gallantly Announce "We Are Women"
And To People Around The World, This Message

This Battle I Must Fight, Now Becomes We
For We'll Stand United And Never Alone
Like Marching Into War As Women Soldiers
Much Like Our Sisters Of The Past, Had Known

If I Should Die, And Never To Awaken
I Will Go Knowing I Fought Till The Finish
I Lived With No Disappointments
And My Strength Did Never Diminish

This Battle I Must Fight
I'll Not Hide My Body In Shame
From The World Of Billions
And Here, My Dignity I Will Reclaim

I Am Beautiful For The World To See
However, The Way I Appear
You Accept Me As I Am
Without Prejudice Or Fear

RENO AND I

A White Poodle I Simply Adore
A Ball Of Fluff, Bought At Eight Weeks
With Puppy Eyes Just Looking At Me
Take Take, Take Me, As If Trying To Speak

She Whimpered Upon Picking Her Up
It Was Dead Set, She Now Belonged To Me
I Didn't Want A Dog, Somehow, I Was Stuck
Now Completes My Family

Wagging Her Tail In An Excited Joy
We Welcomed Her Home To Settle In
I Named Her Reno, So Aptly Suited
Her Life Anew, Just Waiting To Begin

Licking My Hand, As If To Say Thank You
She Took To Me And Hubby In An Instant
A New Family Member, This Reno And I
Was Always Close, Never At A Distant

A Loyal Little Pooch, Was Always By My Side
Never Went Anywhere Without Me There
Follows Me Around, Whether The Toilet Or Bath
I Really Know, She Really Did Care

Reno And I, A Companion For Ever
Lived A Good Life, And Yes Spoilt Rotten
But She Was My Baby, On Four Legs
Whatever She Wanted, She Had Gotten

Now, Dakota, A Sister Of Hers
A Bull Mastiff, Were The Best Of Friends
She's Now Passed Away, Would Run And Play Together
Stayed With her Till Her Very End

Reno Did Really Miss Her So
Whined For Days, Kept Looking For Her
She Was Too Young To Understand, She
Went To A Better Place, Where Other Dogs Were

A Little Hoarder This Reno Was
Hid Her Biscuits Under My Covers
Perhaps For When, Winter Came
She Knew For Certain, They Were Hers

Crumbs, All Over The Sheet
Now To Clean Them Up
A Messy Little Thing
For A Ball Of Fluff, This Little Pup

The Years Have Grown, And So Has She
And Still A Mummy's Little Dog
Will Sleep In My Bed, Rather Then On The Floor
I Swear At Time, You Could Hear Her Talk

Reno, Was More Of A Child
Requiring All The Full Attention
Whimpers When She's Ever Left Alone
If She Could Smile, It Would Be Infectious

I Should Have Called Her Angel
But That Was Already Been Taken
Her Character Was Of Grace
I Know At Times, I Was Mistaken

She Had Manners, Unlike Any Other Dog
Fed Off The Table, To Eat My Food
Only Things Missing, The Knife And Fork
Sorry To Say, These, I Did Not Include

Reno, Was Almost Human You Might Say
What's Was Mine, Was Hers, Including My Bra
Often Seen Laying, Top Of It, Or Over Her Head
Thought This Was A Funny Ha Ha

Like A Fashion Designer, Just Loved My Clothes
Sat On Top Of Them, Lying On My Bed
Cosily She Would Nestle Up Beside Me
Sometimes On My Shoulder, Her Tiny Little Head

A Funny Sight To See, Wanting To Be Fed,
Bearing Weight On Two Legs
Front Paws In A Sparring Motion
When Often, For Food She Would Beg

With Child Like Character, A Picky, Stubborn Pup
By My Side, Never Apart, Always Spoilt
Wouldn't Change Any Of This
Even Though Possessive To A Point

Reno And I Were Inseparable, Even Bathing Time
Would Often Lick Me Up, Be In Bed, Or On Lounge
Wherever The Mood Took Her
She Was There, Always Around

Many Times, Got My Attention, There Was A Few
Would Remove The Remote From Its Place
With Flick And A Nudge
But In The End, It Was Her, I Would Embrace

Yeah Reno, Was A Clingy Type Of Dog
Like Shit To The Diaper, She Would Stick
Turn Around, There She Was
But Chase Her, She Was Quick

Be Weary, She's Always Lurking
You Couldn't See Her, But She Was
Somewhere, You Could Feel Her Presence
I Knew She Loved Me, Just Because

She Sits On The Window Ledge Upon Arrival
Pulling In My Driveway, There She Sat
Tail Waggling, Watching My Every Move
Thought It Kinda Cute, At That

I Know She Will Pass Away One Day
And Will Dearly Miss Her Charm
Can Never Be Replaced For Money Or Love
Will Remember Always Her Tender Warmth

She Is Some Seventeen Years, Give Or Take
Went Into Operation, Hoping She Wouldn't Die
I Will Miss Her So Much
But Always Will Be Knowing, It Was Reno And I

HAUNTED MANSION

Beneath The Thunderous Skies
Upon The Murky Peated Hills
The Ground, Cold In The Sludged Mire
While Corpses, Below The Surface, Fills

A Silhouette In The Distance
As Lightening Crashes Upon An Ancient Fortress
Shadows Extend In The Dense Dark Night
As Your Fear, You Try To Suppress

This House, Where Nobody Dwells
There, A Family Was Hung, Now Seek Vengeance
The Tower Bells Alarm Spirits Of Unmarked Graves
And Ghastly Corpses Nearby Danced

Ravaging Into The Night, While
Flesh From Their Bodies Dangled
And Maggots, In A Frenzy Scavenged
Off Their Limbs That Dragged

One Can Hear Howling Wolves
In Packs, Something Ominous About To Happen
Skies, Blanketed By Swarms Of Locusts
Awaiting An Apocalypse To Begin

Slowly You Approach
Opening The Door As It Creaks
All Around, Dimly Lit Rooms
Where Nobody Disturbs The Peace

Cobwebbed And Dusty, Chandeliers Hung
Its Crystals Catching The Faintest Glimmer.
It's Like Into Another Dimension
Or Looking Into A Reflective Mirror

This Mansion, Haunted
A Reminder Of Those Many Years Ago
When The Departed, Here, Used To Dwell
Well, Not That Anybody Did Know

In The Haunted Mansion,
Whispers Echoes, Getting Louder
I Can Feel The Forces With A Biting Chill
Before Me A Spectral Figure, A Halo Surrounds Her

She Moves With A Stealth Motion
Gliding Through The Air
Blanked Out Eyes, In An Empty Socket Lit In Neon Green
Piercing, Looking At Me, Staring At Her, I'd Not Dare

Fear, Within Me Ignites
So Badly Wanting To Leave, But Helpless
I'm Shivering In This Cold Atmosphere
My Anxiety I Must Strive To Suppress

As Sweat From My Brows Drips,
Like A Prisoner With No Escape
Frightened By Their Closeness
And What If, My Soul, They Would Take

I Can Feel Their Sinister Shadows Around,
Their Presence Consuming The Light
I'm Not Meant To Be Freed From Here
Nor Will I Sleep Into The Night

In Every Room, Where Portraits Hung
Eyes, Moving, Watching
Every Step That I Make, My Heart Beating
To The Point Of Near Stopping

There's Silence, As The Whispers Fade
But Still The Dread Remains
I Continue As A Captive In My Own Mind
But My Sanity, Must Try To Retain

These Eerie Screams, Noises Resounding
The Sounds Of Shackled Chains
From Wall To Wall Spirits Scampering
To Find A Way Out, Or For Eternity, Here To Remain

A Shivering, Spine Chilling Wind Outside
Alert The Rustling Leaves,
Overwhelmed By This Unearthly Feeling
Taking My Soul, Like Vicious Thieves

And Outside, Beyond The Trees
Shapeshifters, Horned Demons
Patrol The Mansion
Came To Earth, Cast Down From The Heavens

They Are Never Seen, Never Heard
These, The Lingering Shadows
Their Presence Felt In The Chilled Air
A Feeling Of Uncertainly Within Me Grows

The Mansion Breathes
A Sigh Of Ancient Sorrows
Comes To Life As The Moon Rises
Until The Morning, When The Cock Crows

Dare You Enter The Haunted Mansion?
Be Wary Of What Lies Beyond Those Doors
There Is No Turning Back
If Trapped In Hell, Beneath Those Creaking Floors

LOVE UNREQUITED

A Love Story Beginning, Boy Sees Girl
At A High School Graduation
All Dressed Up, Trying To Impress
Finds Himself In An Awkward Situation

You See, He Is Kinda Shy
And Is New In This Ball Park
Plenty Of Players Vying For The Same Spot
Wanting To Meet Someone, To Make A Mark

With Confidence Lacking, Has A Drink
He's Underage, So, Just A Soda Pop
He Spies Her In A Romantic Gaze
Heart Beating Faster, Then Seems To Stop

Catching His Breath, An Additional Soda
He's Seen Her Before, Built A Fantasy Around Her
Only, Now The Courage, No More Imagining
In His Journal, Would Write Her Poetry In Verse

As He Walks Up, She Is Approached By Another
And A Peck Upon Her Rosy Cheeks
With His Head Hanging Down,
Walks To His Seat, As He Fails To Speak

Just Voices To His Head, Thinking
"I Wanted Her, Like Quenching For Thirst"
The Music Plays, They Get Up To Dance
From A Distance Watching, Thinking He Was First

"It's Now Or Never, Here's Your Chance"
A Voice Inside His Head
Gets Up, Shoulders Back, With A Sturdy Stride
"Mind If I Cut In", Her Face Just Turning Red

"Hi! I'm Daniel, Hope You Don't Mind
I Have Been Watching You Awhile"
But Was Afraid To Ask
I Was Captivated By Your Smile

"By The Way I'm Janet, And Nice To Meet You"
I've Seen You Around, But Always Busy
Head In The Books At School
But Never Thought Much Really

"But I Must Tell You, I Have A Boyfriend"
He Couldn't Make It Tonight
But I'll Be Happy To Just Sit And Chat
If That Is All Right"

"Sure, That Would Be Fine I Guess"
Deep Down Within, His Heart Sank
Perhaps In A Jealous Rage
Not Sure What To Think, His Mind Blank

I Longed For Her, But Now Not Reciprocated
"I Guess I Now Know About Love Unrequited
Always Wondered "Why Me"
Never Before, Has My Heart Ever Ignited

With A Passion, A Desire To Share My Affection
"Was It Really Love" I Thought,
Or Just And Obsession
With Someone I Thought About, A Lot

We Chatted The Night Away And
Danced Some More
Had To Accept There Was No Romance
Though My Body, For Her I Longed As Ever Before

Like A Lovesick Puppy, I Pined Within
Faking It With A Smile, She Couldn't See Through
It Was A Game Of Pretending
Only I Really Knew

I Read About Teenage Crushes
She Wanted A Friendship, And I, Something Further
But I Had To Accept What I Had
And Now, Well! I Couldn't Tell Her

She's Now Found Another, To Take My Place
Not That I Had Her Anyway
Yes! I Was Smitten, Perhaps Came On Too Strong
I Found No Reason, To Really Stay

"Sorry, Janet, It's Getting Really Late
And Mother Is Picking Me Up Soon"
Had To Lie, Couldn't Face It Any Longer
But Told Her Would See Her Tomorrow Afternoon

I Didn't Like Pretending, I Was Fine
Was I Riddled With Some Noxious Plague?
I Was Ever So Nice To Her,
Perhaps Now Thinking, My Intentions Were Vague

Love Unrequited, I Now Got A Taste Of
It Wasn't Meant To Be, I Realised
Feeling Sorry For Myself, Self- Pity
But I Must Admit, The Evening Did Open My Eyes

She Was A Nice Girl, I Will Admit
But Have Since, Met With A Different Girl
Letters Of Affection I Would Write, Shirley
Was Her Name, But I Called Her Shirl

But None, Ever Came Back
Was I Wasting My Time Again?
I Refused To Believe That, Coz! Getting To Know Her
Was Just A Matter Of When?

A PROMISE

A Vision Before Me, Of A Life Together
A Promise I'll Make, To Take By Your Hand
And On One Knee, Pledge To My Vows
A Life We'll Share, Is That I've Planned

To The Aisle Of Wedded Bliss, They Call It
We'll Announce To Honour Each Other
To Battle, With Whatever Came Our Way
In Sickness And In Health, Looking After One Another

You Made A Promise, When You Said "I Do"
I Need Assurance From You, Right Now
You Will Never Desert Or Treat Me Wrong
I Cannot Imagine, How You Would, Or How

We Had Our Quarrels A Lover's Spat
Then Still Young, Didn't Know Better
But We Were Still Learning, At Understanding Life
Getting To Know, Each Other Clearer

How Could I Believe You, With A Love Forsaken?
Hiding Behind The Deceit And Lies
I Don't Want To Let Go, What We Have
I Want To Wake, And Before Me, Your Eyes

I Need You To Be My Pillar Of Strength
A Shoulder On Which To Rely Upon
By My Side, To Catch Me When I Fall
To Dearly Miss You, When You're Gone

Our Paths Will Always Be Tested
And Temptation Will Set In
Together We Are Strong With A Bond United
With Depth That Will Come From Within

Make Me A Promise, When I Perish This Earth,
To Die In Your Arms Wrapped Around
And Be Remembered As I Am,
When I Have Risen, To Heaven Bound

YOU'VE ALWAYS BEEN

From The Time I Was Conceived

To The Time I Entered This

World

You've Always Been There

And Right Beside, For

Me

Watched Over, In My

First Steps I Had

Taken

It Was Your Gentle Voice

I Came To Have

Heard

"You Can Do It, Baby, You're Doing Well,"

So Great To

See

Hold On, Just A While Longer

I Know You Won't Be

Beaten

You've Always Been, The Person

Who You Are

Today

Giving Every Part Of You,

Asking Nothing In

Return

Like My Shadow, Being There
Whenever I Needed, You've Always
Been
You Never Gave Up,
And Never Turned Me
Away
You Were Always Ready To Teach
I Was Much Eager To
Learn
You Gave Your All, Without
Complaint, Giving Your Heart
Within
When It Stormed, You Gave Shelter
Protected From The
Rain
I Was Scared, But Never
Felt Rejected Or
Alone
You Gave Strength, Helped
Fight My Inner
Demons
The Courage To Battle Adversity
That In My Life
Remained

You've Been The Force And
Foundation On Which Your Love
Is Etched In
Stone
Good Days, Bad, There's Been Many
But Was Always Near, Never
Distanced
Felt Down. When I Failed
You Picked Me Up And Assured All Be
Fine
You Smiled My Way And
Said That You Were
Proud
I Knew Then, It Was Upon
You, That I Could Always
Lean
Knowing You'll Always Be There
And So Lucky To Call You
Mine
No Other Person, I'd Share
My Life, No Other, Have Ever I
Found
You're A Mother, A
Friend, That You've Always
Been

NOTHING ELSE MATTERED

We Were Young, And When

Dreams Were

Shattered

But We Grew Up With

Heads On Our

Shoulders

We Shrugged Our Future Off

Coz Every Day Was Like Our

Last

Finding Our First Crush

Those Days, Nothing Else

Mattered

I Met Her In The Playground,

Playing With Barbie, And I, With Toy

Soldiers

But Lacked The Courage

To Kiss Her, Too Afraid To

Ask

Nothing Else Mattered

When Your Heart Skips A

Beat

You Fumble To Talk,

The Words Just Turn Out

Wrong

As I Watched Her Smile
Butterflies
Flew
Walking Up To Her, Words Memorized
"Would You Like To
Meet"
She Hesitated To Answer,
But Her Response, Seemed
Long
Her Eyes Met Mine, I Thought
I Had A Chance, This I
Knew
It Wasn't Long, We Joined Hands
And Strolled Up To
McDonalds
A Date To Remember,
Licking On Those Strawberry Gelato
Cones
She Ate My Fries, And I
Pulled Her
Hair
She Got Mad And Started To Pout,
Out Of Nowhere Hurled
Insults

I Apologised And Said Sorry
And From My Hand Gave
Two Raspberry
Scones
She Smile, And Said
You Are Forgiven. But Don't You Ever
Dare.
I Ring Her To This
Day, And Often Thinks Of
Me
Remembering Those Times
We Frolicked And
Cried
We Are Old And Somewhat Wiser
I Was Saddened, She Was Leaving, I Had
Heard
I Asked Her If She Would Stay
Longer, Or To Meet Up, If Was
Free
I Couldn't Tell Her I Was Really
Hurting Deep
Inside
Those Days Or Our Youth
Came Crashing Through, When I Knew
Then, When Nothing Else
Mattered

BACK IN TIME

In A Time, In A Place, In A Far Distant Plain
We Travelled Beyond The Stars
Back To What Was
Back In Time, That We Made Ours

We Turned Back The Seconds Of Time
As If It Stood Still, For A Moment
No Past, No Forthcoming, Only The Here And Now
The Future, We Couldn't Prevent

Like Aliens Travelling Back In Time
To A Distant Planet, Some Celestial Sphere
Into Another Fourth Dimension
Like A Galactic Pioneer

Back In Time, Man Have Thrived
In Pursuit Of Adventure And Escapade,
To Journey Into The Unknown
At Times With Their Lives They Paid

What Lay In The Past, Remains Truly Buried
Beneath, At The Mercy Of Time
Serves A Reminder Of How We Were.
Fought The Obstacles, We Had To Climb

If I Could, One Day Travel
Back In Time, To A Time That Was
There'll Be Nothing That I Would Change
Knowing of the damages, it may cause

THE ASHES

I Dreamt Of You The Other Day
Almost Felt Like You Were Away,
Gone
You Seemed Upset, No One
To Hear Your
Verses
And Cried At The Thought
Of Never Seeing Me
Again
As I Approached To Give A Hug
You Moved Away, Kinda
Withdrawn
I Knew For A Moment
You Were Hurting Under A Toughened
Surface
I Told You, Id Be Back
Just Didn't Know
When
The Visions Seemed Everlasting
But, Was As If, I Was Living
This
"Who Would Listen To My Poetry"
Crying On My
Chest

I Assured You, Your Heart Will

Always Be With

Mine

In That Short Moment,

Our Lips Met, Then We

Kissed

I Knew Your Deepest Feeling

You Had

Expressed

As Only This Type Of Love

Can Be

Defined

"Honey! I Will Always Be Your

Inspiration To

Write"

The Simplest, Or Moving, Yet Deepest

That You Can

Imagine

They'd Be Written From Your

Heart, That's Really Of

Value

Whatever You Compile, I

Know, Will Be Just

Right

This Will Always Be

Your Undying

Passion

And Will Forever Remind

Me Of

You

And If By Some Ill- Luck I Will

Perish And

Die

Please Scatter My Ashes To The Wind

And Your Poems To Comfort

Me

I Will Guide You In Spirit

That You'll Never Walk

Alone

You Told Me You'd Miss Me

And Wouldn't Know What To

Do

I Held Your Hand, Brought You

Closer, Looked Into Your

Eyes

From That Instance Your

Love Held The

Key

I Woke Up That Morning,

My Body In A Cold

Sweat

Lying Beside Me, My Hand

Upon Your

Chest

"Are You Awake Honey,
Had The Weirdest
Dream"
It Was Something
I Will Never
Forget
Didn't Want Me Leaving, No-One
Listening To Your Poems, Looking So
Depressed
I Am Happy, Was Just A Dream
Wasn't As It Is, Or Really
Seems

THE HARDEST THING

Filled With Lingering Regrets,
From The Early Moments Of Birth
Until Life's Very End
Perish To The Afterlife From This Earth

A Mother, Gives Birth To Her Child
Knowing One Day, It Too shall leave The Nest,
Letting Go, For It To Grow Up
But Always Wanting, For Them, The Best

The Hardest Thing, Before Her Eyes
Maturing, To Be an Adult
Moving Out, Getting Married
Then Who Will They Consult

Fend for Themselves or learning From Failures
Getting Back Up, When At Once they Fail
They'll face the trials and tribulations
But through adversity, their strength prevails

Thriving as they Leave their Youth Behind
Will Always Be The Hardest Thing
One Day To Wake Up, Suddenly Wrinkled, Old
Never Knowing What The Future May Bring

Recalling The Teenaged Years
Sacrifices Were Made
The Hardest Thing, I Endured the Pain
A friendship, that Was Betrayed

Since Those Years Have Passed
I've Forgiven And Forgotten
But truly, never broke passed the heartaches
When Feeling Depressed, Down Trodden

The Hardest Thing, Accepting Our Faults
Or The Dark Past, That Looms Above
In Secrecy, We Turned Our Backs
And Walked Away From Those We Loved

I Can Still Remember To This Day
With A Shattered Heart…
That I Wore upon My Sleeve
On That Day, We Drifted Apart

She Was The One That Got Away
From My Grasp, From My Clutches
Was The Hardest Thing, Letting Her Go
When I Couldn't Hold, Anything My Heart Touches

But So Many Loves Enter Our Lifetimes
Many That Will Come, Then Soon to Move Away
staying for the moment, then disappear
Leaving On Their Parted Ways

STUFF IT

Times In My Life I Have Felt So Low
A World Filled With People
But Never Those Close Enough
Always Above Me, Never Their Equal

You Asked If I Am Ok
But Do You Genuinely Care
Care Enough To Worry If I Truly Was,
Or just Pretending I'm Really There?

I Don't Care Anymore, So Stuff It
Giving Up Trying, What's The Use Of Caring
Or Continue, Carrying On
When All You See In Me, Is The Hate I'm Wearing

Stop Asking If I'm Fine
Or Concerned For My Wellbeing
You Just Make believe, You Are My Friend
It's Not Your Sympathy, I Am Seeking

Stuff It, With All Your Lies And BS
You've Numbed My Senses
Into Believing You Were Real
Hard To Know Now, What A Friend Is

My Best Was Never Good Enough,
Wiping My Hands Clean, So Stuff It
I Always Tried To Please You
But You Found This Hard To Admit

I Pretend To Wear A Smile,
But Only Hurtful Tears, Do I Cry
And Still, You Question If I'm Just Right
It's Like Persecution, And Still I Wonder Why

A Slave, Is How You Think Of Me?
The Way You Manipulate, Control
With Lies And Deception, My Feelings, Hard To Preserve
And Then You Came And Captured My Soul

You Gained My Trust, Then Threw It Away,
Abuse It, Should I Bother
When You Don't Give A Damn
You Stripped Me Of Dignity Took Away My Honour

How Can I Move Forward?
When You Are Right Behind
Controlling My Very Essence
My Life You Stole Away And Robbed Me Blind

Hearing You Talking Behind My Back
Fingers Pointing, Throwing Blame
To All That, I Say Stuff It
But It's Not On Me, You're Putting In Shame

My Mind, In Anguish, Turmoil
With Lingering Thoughts Scattered
I'm Going Beyond The Threshold Of Caring
And Found Nothing, That Really Mattered

I Can't Put Any Efforts, When You Tell
Me You Don't Care…
Or Find Reasons To Love,
When It's Your Lies, I Cannot Bear

I Wanted To Know What Emotions Were
Only To Be Shackled By Lies And Deception
Is There Any Truth To What You Say Or Have You?
Too Been Blinded By Rejection?

When Like A Puppet You Played Me
Pulling Strings, In All Directions
I Cannot Handle Much More, So Stuff It
Never Knowing, Just Where I'm At

I've Stopped Worrying What You, Others
Think Of Me, I Can Only Aspire To Be Me
I Don't Need Your Approval
To Who I Choose To Be

When I Look Into The Mirror
Who Do I See, A Man Alone
Living Up To Someone's Expectation
But Never My Own.

Those Who Have Instilled In Me Self Doubt
My Thoughts Are What Matters Now
Never Will My Self Esteem Be Lowered
This, I Shall Never Allow

I Have Many Flaws, Mistakes Aplenty
I Just Want To Be Who I Once Was
Not That Person I Have Become
I Want To Cry, Scream, For No Just Cause

I've Gratified People All My Life
When Shall I Start Pleasing Me?
I'm On The Verge Of Tears
That No-One Around, Can See

Whatever You Think Of Me
Is Of No Relevance
Deep Down, You Truly Hurt, Used To Think,
Your Friendship Served Importance

I've Risen From The Ashes
From The Ground, For So Long Buried
My Life, Now Call Mine
And To Better Prospects, I Will Be Carried

OPEN BOOK

Like A Mystery Novel, Or An
Adventure Cruise,
My Life Is Certainly Not That
But One, I Cannot Refuse

Or Upon A Roller Coaster, In A Theme Park
Every Corner, Every Bend
My Being, Seemingly Twirls To Nowhere
Waiting For It To Reach The End

Like An Open Book, Waiting To Be Read
It Stands Upon A Library Shelf,
With Words, Some Yet To Be Written
That I Must Do Myself

With Thoughts I've Come To Convey
Though I Know, May Sound Obscure
And Words Will Disappear In Translation
These, Within Myself, Find Hard To Endure

I Am An Open Book, With Pages To Be Read
There Are No Hidden Agendas
So, Feel Free To Read The Many Chapters
I Trust You Won't Be Offended

Knowing Who I Am
Can Perhaps Guide Me, To Who I'll Be
I May Be Different, Yes That Is True
Cannot Promise You'll Love Me… Ain't No Guarantee

I Am An Open Book, That Much Is Real
I Don't Pretend To Be Who I'm Not
I Bleed Like You Do, Cry The Same Tears
But I Always Give, What I've Got

It May Not Be Much
Am Always Happy To Share
Expecting Nothing In Return
Friendship, That I Ask, If You Truly Do Care

I May Look Tough,
But Wear My Heart On My Sleeve
When All That's Important To Me
Would Die, Leaving Me To Grieve

I'm An Open Book, With Nothing In Between
Not Afraid To Give Out My Heart
To Show Who I Am, I Laugh, I Cry
Yet Still, From Me You Will Depart

May Say Things, I Don't Mean
At Times Through, Anger And Spite
With Emotion Filled Eyes Tearing
Real, As These Words I Write…

Like An Open Book,
Will Speak My Mind
What You See Is What You Get
No Other Like Me, Is That You'll Find

I Have No Secrecy, Just Ask
As Sure As The Sky Is Blue,
Or The Day Turns To Night
Trust Me Dear Friend All This Be True

There Can Be Darkness Feeling Lonely
Where Light Can Never Shine
Happiness Is Only A Give And Take
But Why Oh Why, Can I Not Make Mine

That Script The Stands Upon A Library Shelf
The Story Of My Life, As An Open Book
You Want To Get To Know Me Better
Heed Not, And Take A Closer Look

If You're Willing To Know Me
Read On The Pages
What Will Unfold,
Through The Varying Different Stages

ONE MORE CHANCE

This Maybe Just Another Miss You Verse
That I've Written Just For You Alone
When I Cannot Bear To Know You're Not There
How I Think About You As My Own

One More Time To Carry On.
Just One More Chance To Undo The Wrong
I Want To Embrace In Your Love
For I Know Together, We Are Strong

With My Arms Around You Tightly
To Feel Your Pounding Heart Within
The Heat Between Us Rises
That's The Way It's Always Been

When I Heard Your Voice In
Calmness Of The Night
It Was Then I Realized You And I
Were Meant To Be, This, Would Make It Right

Just One More Chance To Show
I Care And Let Water Under The Bridge Flow
A New Beginning Darling Can Be Ours
And Emotions Between Us Will Grow

I'm Sorry It Had To Be This Way
If I Could Pick The Stars From This Universe
I'd Give Them To You, To Brighten
Your Darkest Nights And Release Me From This Curse

Just One More Chance To Make
The Wrongs Right, And Let Me Live Again
Please Tell Me How
If Only I Would Know When

I Do Believe In Miracles
And Still Believe In Us Together
Even Though The Paths Have Been Rocky,
We Triumphed, Whatever The Weather

The Journeys We Travelled Amidst Ups And Downs
Along Those Bumpy Crackled Roads
Lead Us To The Here And Now
Promising To Carry Each Other's Loads

Don't Let Our Dreams Be Shattered.
Don't Let The Love We've Shared Just Disappear
One More Chance To Salvage A Lost Love
And How Wrong To Forget, What Brought Us Here

Wherever The Streams Of Life May Take Us.
I Want To Share Whatever I Have, And Give To You
Every Moment, Every Waking Hour
More Than I Ever Knew

Memories Came Crashing Through
That First Day We Met
I Spied You From A Distance, Far Away
That Moment Would Not Let Me Forget

How Your Hair, In That Summer Breeze
Caught My Eye That Day
You Couldn't Tell I Was Watching
When You Turned To Look, I Quickly Turned Away

Those Memories Of You, Quickly Became Etched
In My Brain And Still Today There Is No Other
I Pledged To Make You My All
Just One More Chance, I'll Never Ask Another

Just One More Chance
To Take Back The Words I Had Wrongly Spoken
Or The Things I Unjustly Did
I Cannot Understand, Why Our Love Should Be Broken

ANNOYING SISTERS

We Grew Up Like Two Peas In A Pod
Yes Inseparable At Times
I Was A few years Older Than Her, She
Was My Younger Sister, My Partner In Crime?

If That Wasn't Bad Enough
We Still Shared Each Other's Diapers
And Mother, Wasn't Impressed
Yes! She Was Annoying, But Never A Fighter

We Played Tricks And I Got Away With It
She Would Pull My Hair, And I Would Cry
She Got Away With It
But I Would Always Wonder Why

Come Dressing Up Time
She Would Always Wear My Bra
But I Got The Last Laugh
It Was Way Too Big For Her, Ha Ha

We Fought Like Cats And Dogs
Claws Came Gashing, Then Hair Came Pulled
It Was Free For All, No Hold Bars
Competitive, Like Any Sister Would

She Would Stuff It With Socks, Made No Difference
Hers Were Fried Eggs, Just Had To Say
But I Really Had To Laugh
It's Ok Sis, Don't Cry, Yours Will Be Big Some Day

Yeah! My Sister Can Be Annoying
As Messy As She Was, But Had Her Back
Would Stand Up For Me, When I Couldn't
But Courage, She Never Lacked

I Have Another Sister, But She Is Still Little
The Peace Maker In The Family
The Apple In My Father's Eye
Getting Away With Murder, She Began Early

Now I Have Two Annoying Sisters
If One Wasn't Enough, Twice The Trouble
Pinching My Things, I Would Get Their Blame
I'd Swear They Were My Double

It's Okay Though, I Was Much Bigger
I Would Sit On Them, And Chuckle
Mummy!! They Would Yell Out
But In The End, With Them I Would Snuggle

Comes That Time Of The Month
It's Those Essentials We'll Get To Share
One Size Fits All, So They Tell Me
Only If One Is Handy, And With Me, They Can Spare

It's Hard To Imagine Life Without
My Darling Annoying Sisters
And Their Crazy Little Mixed-Up Ways
Why Couldn't I Just Have Brothers

Oh! And I Forgot That I Do
But This Is Not About Them
Tis About My Sisters
And I Have, Again, Two Of Em

Their Tongue Poking, Really Gets To Me
They Pull My Hair, And Their Smart Alec Ways
Would I Change Any Of That, I Probably Would Not
But Then Again, Those Were The Younger Days

I'm Like A Mother To Them Now
When They Need My Help, I Will Be There
They Look Up To Me, For I Am Much Taller
But Seriously Though, For Them I Really Care

My Sisters Can Be Annoying
Wouldn't Change Them For The World
They Add Humour To My Life
And It's Their Respect; I Will Have Earned

WISH ME LUCK

Wish Me Luck, As I'll
Soon Be On My
Way
I've Paid My Dues, That Time
Has Come, I'll Say
Good-Bye
As I Lay In My Bed With
Each Breathless
Moment
Please Don't Cry, We'll
Be Together Soon, One
Day
Then I Will Remember,
With Me You Stood
By
When Down The Aisle,
Our Vows We Had
Spoken
Wish Me Luck When I Go,
Shed No
Tears
I Will Go, Won't Be Back,
But I'll Watch Over
You

From Up There Above
The Clouds Of
White
To Live With The Angels
And The Man
Upstairs
When My Time On Earth
Has Ended, Or
Due
Ill Pray You'll Think Of
Me, Please Never Lose
Sight
Till We Meet In Due Course
Dear Friend, Wish
Me Luck As I
Go
There'll Soon Come A Time,
Our Paths Will Again
Meet
So, Till Then, Please Share
Me Your
Smile
And Hold My Hand As You
Did, Those Years
Ago

And Made My Life, Defined
And So
Complete
I Know I Must Go, Wish I Didn't
Just A Moment Longer, A Little
While
And When I'm Carried Out The Door
Wish Me Luck, Just Wave
Good bye

LEAVE, WHAT WAS YESTERDAY

When The Morning Has Dawned

And The Sun Has

Risen

Look Out The Window

And Embrace The

Day

Leave What Was Yesterday

Enjoy What The Lord Has

Given

To You, A Child Of His World, And

At His Arms Reach, You Will

Stay

A Moment Passes, Never

Lose Track Of Your

Time

Before Your Eyes

Visions Cascade, Of Where You Have

Been

What's To Come, Cannot

Be Determined, Without Those Mountains

Climbed

And In The End, Problems

Aren't As Hard, As Once, May Have

Seemed

Leave, What Was Yesterday
For Today Is In The
Making
Savour The Moments
That Will Soon Be Your
Tomorrow
When You Grasp A Fleeting Moment
Possibilities, Are
In For The
Taking
You Can Take Hold Now,
To Rid The Angst And Future
Sorrows
Leaving What Was Yesterday
As No Days Are Left In
Concrete
No Paths Have Been Paved
No Doors Yet To
Open
You've Only One Opportunity
Fulfil Your Life
Complete
Never Look Back, With Regrets
And Never Look Back, With Words
Unspoken

PHYSICAL ATTRACTION

She Was A Senior At An Elite High School
I Was Sixteen That Year, She was Nineteen
During The Lunch Hour, Sitting By Herself
Most Gorgeous Creature, I Had Ever Seen

From That Moment I Laid Eyes On Her
An Instant Physical Attraction
I Was Too Shy To Even Talk To Her
But Had To Take Drastic Action

To Build Up The Courage.
My Heart Racing, Skipping A Beat
Palms Sweating, My Throat Became Dry
I Had To Think Of A Way To Meet

I See Her Reading A Book
She Looks My Way, I Turn The Other Direction
I Turn Around To See Her Smiling At Me
There, In Front Of Me, My Idea Of Perfection

I Inch My Way To Where She Is Seated
I Can Feel The Blush Running To My Face
In A Provocative Way, She Bites Her Lips
A Fresh Mint In My Mouth, Just In Case

She Closes Her Book, And Says "Hi!"
I Begin To Stammer, My Words Get Caught
"Hi Hi" She Smiles Again, I Smile Back
"I'm Lisa" Hi! I'm Ahhh!" Too Nervous That I Forgot

I Cringed With Shame, She Said "don't be shy"
I Sat Next To Her, We Just Idle Chatted
About Everything And Nothing
Wasn't Important, I Was With Her, That's, What Mattered

I Hadn't Been With Girls Before, Let Alone A
Pretty Looking One. Blonde Hair, Blue Eyes
Curves In The Right Places
She Lived Two Doors Down, To My Surprise

"How Come I've Never Seen You Before"
You Live So Close" She Suggests
"I Was Always Shy Growing up in Life"
Never Went Out, Just Stayed Home To Reflect

Twiddling Her Hair, Moistening Her Lips
Don't Know Much About Body Language
But, My Intuition, Says I'm Doing Well
And Thinking, "Her And I Can Really Manage"

The Lunch Bell, Sirens, Time To Go Back
I Carry Her Books, And Exchange Phone Contact
Before We Parted Our Ways That Afternoon, I asked
"Can We Meet Again?" She Replies, "I'd Like That"

The Rest Is History
We Are Married And She's Expecting Twins
Hard To Believe, I Was Hooked By Her Physical Attraction
Now There, Our Next Generation Begins.

CAN WE START OVER AGAIN

I've Lived A Life Of

Wine Women And

Song

I Failed To Cherish

What We Had, When I

Played Around, Acted The

Fool

I'm Trying To Tell

You, My Actions Were Terribly

Wrong

I Know Deep Inside Within

My Intentions Were

Cruel

Can We Start Over Again?

I'll Be The Man You've Dreamt

Of

I Know It May Never Happen

But Can We Give It A

Chance

I Took You For Granted

When You Gave Me Your

Love

Deserted You, And All We Had,

Killed Our Passion, Our

Romance

Can We Start Over Again?
Igniting The Flames Of The Fire
Within
I Don't Want To Forget
The Love We
Knew
But Hope, In My Heart
That Your Love Again I Can
Win
And Together Forever, Resurrect
A Love That Once We
Grew
I Know My Scars
Will Heal, But For Now Go
On Living This
Lie
I Cannot Pretend I Don't
Love You, When Deep Inside
You Know I
Care
I'll Keep On Trying To
Find You Till That Day I
Die
Then I'll Know The Pain Will
Heal and With Time Will Mend-
Repair

Can We Start Over Again?
To Free The Knife That Digs My
Sides
I Cannot Pretend That
It Doesn't
Hurt
There In My Heart
I Feel That Your Love Has
Died

THIS POEM

I've Written Something You Might Like

It Really Isn't Much, Just A Little

Poem

It May Seem Simple And It

May Not

Rhyme

But It Is Written From The Heart

And Hope, That Really

Matters

At Times Found It Hard, To Write

Not Knowing What It Will

Become

It May Not Be A Best Seller

Many Won't Read, But Time Will Tell, Just

Time

Ideas Of What To Write

All Over The Place, Seemingly

Scattered

This Poem, Words Upon Words

Scrambling For Inspiration

To What Will

Proceed

"My Dearest", Might Be A Good

Way To

Start

"I Write This Poem Especially,
Just For
You"

You're Everything A Man Could
Want, Most Certain, Everything I
Need

This Poem, With You I Will Share
Written Deeply From My
Heart

Reading, You Will Find, That
What's Written, You'll Find To Be
True

My Emotions, Through This Poem
What Better Way To
Express

Through Words I Have Compiled
May Sound A Little
Childish

Like A Teenager Finding His First Love
With A Girl, That Romance Will
Bloom

Will Try To Amuse Her, As
Any Male Will Try To
Impress

And Perhaps Later, Be Granted
His Every
Wish

When Down The Aisle They
Walk As The Newly Bride And
Groom

NATURE'S TREASURES

The Foundation Of Our Existence
The Pillar On Which Life Stands
That Bonds A Mother And Child
As We've Come To Understand

A Silky Negligee To Cover
Nature's Own Hidden Treasures
These Marvelled Creation
With Various Sizes, When Measured

Supple To The Touch
So Be Very Gentle To Admire
They May Weep When Aroused
Hold Them Dear Before They Expire

Smell The Aroma From
Their Scently Perfume
A Lingering Fragrance
That Fills The Room

With Suppleness So
Tender To Touch
The Heart And Soul Of A Woman
This I Know So Much

Cherish Them, They'll
Serve You For Life
Caress Them With Unbroken Desires
Please Them, As You Would Your Wife

These Nature's Treasures
So True To Mesmerize
They'll Send You In A Seductive Trance
Stare Long Enough, Then Be Hypnotised

They Will Truly, Get Their Ways
Never Will You Set Free
So, Picture Them In Their Alluring Glory
I'm Sure We'll Both Agree

That Their Greatness Is Infinite
With A Dimly Speckled Pose
I Much Appreciate Their Beauty
Beneath Their Wearing Clothes

Were Once So Full Of Youth
Time No Longer On Their Sides
Will Travel Down South
And Rest, Where The Belly Button Resides

Nature's Treasures, They Truly Are
Artists Glorify Their Presence
Brush In Hand, Caring For Every Stroke
To Bring Out Their Very Essence

They Respond To The Sweetest Embrace
A Cuddle, A Kiss, Perhaps A Nibbled Treat
A Pinch For Excitement
Will Sure To Raise Up The Heat

Salty Of Taste, Looking Like Pearls
These Natures Treasures Oh So Grand
Like Poetry In Motion, Displayed
But Must Be A Woman To Understand

In The Garden Of Eden
Where She Bore Her Heart
Nature Was A God Send
Life Began Right From That Start

For Generations To Come
They'll Never Fail To Please
The Young And The Old
Nothing Will Be As Grandeur As These

WATER

Above Me, Darken Clouds Gather
The Wind Sails, Will Soon To Rain
Colliding In Fusion, In A Nature's Rage
Below, Swarming Gulls, Its Feeding Time Again

As I Lay Upon The Rocky Shore,
Watching The Crashing Waves
Tides Rolling In, Its Water Splatter
Upon Me, Could Lie Here For Days

The Water Spray Upon Me, Cleansing My Skin
I Welcome Its Revitalising Freshness
My Body, Unaware It Was Drenching
Like Being Anointed, It Blesses Us

As I Watch In Awe, A Rainbow Before Me
Refracting Globules Form
In Nature, Does This Beauty Display
Like Trickery, A Magician Will Perform

But Out To Sea, Once Again Tides Travelled
Its Salty Residue, Leaving My Desires Dis-Contented
Chapped Lips, Needing Something To Quench
To Hit The Spot, My Thirst By Now Collected

This Water, Earth's Liquid Gold
Precious, As That Fountain Of Youth
We'll Strive To Search, This Elixir Of Life
In Searching For The Truth

It Gives Us The Reasons To Live
Like The Air That We Inhale
That We Cannot Exist Without
For Survival To Prevail

From The Mountains To The Valleys,
Lakes And Rivers Did It Stream
Every Droplet To The Ocean Vast
All Around Me, A Glorious Nature Theme

Rain Falls, Pattering Upon A Tin Rooftop
Water Collecting At My Feet Bare
Leaves Floating, Assemble And Gather
Just Watching And Gazing, As I Stare

A New Day Will Dawn, When
The Clouds Will Again Clear
Then Flowers Every Springtime Will Bloom
And Nature's Grandeur Will Reappear

Every Colour Displayed
In All Shades And Various Hues
Their Brightly Splendour
The Crimson, Magenta Or The Royal Blues

Nature Weeps, At The Polluted
Waters It Sees
We Take For Granted What We Have Today
And From This Selfishness, We Must Be Free

Conserve, We Are Constantly Reminded
For Water Sustains Nature, And Nature… Life
Abuse, And Soon To See Our Demise
Will Live Eternally With Ever Endless Strife

No More Rainforest Or Cascading Falls
Nor Water From Which To Drink Or Cleanse
How I'd Long To Swim Again
With My Family And Friends

I'd Want To, On The Beach
See The Water Shimmer, Neath The Twilit Moon
Till The Rivers, The Oceans Run Still
Maybe Tomorrow, Maybe Hopefully Soon

MIRROR

Glazed Tinted Warped
Into Another Dimension
A Reflection Of You Staring At
Me
I See You In The Mirror
Wanting To Pull You
Through
But How Can I Get To You
From The Other Side, To Set You
Free
Can You Not See Me Peering?
How I Long To Be With
You
I Want To Reach Out Through
To The Other
Dimension
I Can Hear Your Voice
Like An Echo Resounding In My
Mind
Cracked Mirror, Your Image
Split Into Thousands, What Is
Real, What Is
Illusion

A Light Shining, That I
Cannot See, My Vision Is Dulled
Near Set Me
Blind
I Want You Here Beside Me
But I Know You Trapped Into Another
Zone
I Want Your Body To Admire
When Lonely Nights Set
In
To Touch You, To Feel The
Warmth, Someone To Call My
Own
I Cannot Lose You Now
To Do All I Can, Your Heart To
Win
There's An Empty Space
Where Besides Me You Once
Stood
Now My Eyes Gaze Your
Reflection In The
Mirror
I Want To Be Immersed
In Your Presence If Only I
Could

Tell Me, What Must I Do
To Get Closer To You, Get
Nearer
I Will Find A Way To Get To
You, If I Can't Be In Your
World
I Will Be In Yours, To Break
Down These Mirror
Walls
And Bring You Back From
Where You've Been
Hurled
Just Whisper My Name
And I'll Be There
At Your Beckoned
Calls

I SPY

A Window Over There,

What Do I

Spy

Lights Dimmed Low

Curtains

Drawn

Opened Wide

A Silhouetted Image

A Pleasure To My

Eye

One Blissful Moment There,

Then It's Suddenly

Gone

She Reappears Through

My 64x Zoom

Binoculars

A Semi Clad, Full Figure

With Pronounced

Curves

My Mind In A Frenzy

Noting Her

Particulars

Sweated Palms, Trembling

Knees With Rattled

Nerves

Light Falls- Into The Next

Room, Shower

Running

A Quick Mirror Glimpse

Moisturising Cream

Applied

Dropping Her Towel,

Disrobing, Her Image,

Stunning

In That Intense Moments

Of Excitement, Frenzied

Images To My

Mind

Shower Bath, Passing

Through Her Shapely

Contours

In Slow Motion, Water

Sprayed Upon The Face I Would

Kiss

Over And Over In My Mind

Going On A Journey With A

Map On Many

Tours

What Could Possibly

Compare To

This

My Vision Became Blurred
Wiping The Sweat From My
Eyes
Fantasies, Mixed Feeling
And Emotions
Overwhelming
Was I In For A Treat?

Or Perhaps A Pleasant
Surprise?
Anticipation Grew, My
Eyes Bulging
Swelling
Urges, Arousals, The Many
I Could Not
Contain
She Looks To My Direction
What Could I
Do
From This Room I
Left, And Could Not
Remain
But Will Always Remember
That Room With A
View

WE ALL BLEED THE SAME

A Newborn Enters The World
With Cries To Alert Of His Presence
Around Him, Faces, Black Or White,
He Knows Of No Difference

No Corruption Has He Learnt
From The Purity Of His Heart
It's The Smiles That He Shares
That Will Set Him Apart

It's The Hatred He Will Come To Learn
No Understanding, Does He Yet Know
Prejudice Will Make Its Way To His Heart
Just As, In History Of Long Time Ago

White Skin, Black Skin Or Yellow
We All Bleed The Same
The World Without Segregation,
Can We Ever, In This World Reclaim

Are We Judged By Our Colour
By Which We Were Born
Tell Me Why We Cannot See Eye To Eye
Or Why, From Our Motherland, Be Torn

What's It Really Like
That We Hate Our Brothers
Our Sisters, And Neighbours Too
Those We Care For, And Many Others

We All Bleed The Same
So Why In Difference We Become Divided
Be In What We Wear
How We Speak, Why Not Be United

We've Walked This Earth
Since Time Began
As Human Learning To Survive
We Reigned, In Accordance With God's Plan

Over The Animals That Roamed
But Now, Over Each Other
Over Those, We've Sacrificed
And The Innocence From Another

Young Lives, At Times Brutally Taken
Butchered Cause They Were Mismatched
Who Followed A Creed, A Religion
And Murderers, Whose Minds, With Racism Etched

We All Bleed The Same
Yet With Fingers Pointing At Me
You Acti Like You're Better
Perhaps One Day, From You, I'll Be Free

When Shall You Open Your Eyes
And Know We All Bleed The Same
Then Realize You Are No Different,
Possibly In Misery, You Shall Fall In Shame

Never Will You Realize, Under Our Skins, We
Share The Same Coloured Blood
We Clothe And Speak In Different Tongues
And Society Will Have Us Judged

For Reasons Being Ignorance,
Resentment, Will Always Loom Around Us
Until We Realize That We All Bleed The Same
And Together As One, Must Learn To Adjust

MY NIGHTMARE VISITORS

I Hear Them Creeping, Scurrying
Feet In Plenty Within My Kitchen Walls
Sweat From My Brows
Seeing More Scrounging Through The Halls

My Mind Pacing, In A Raged-Out Frenzy
Seeing These Nightmare Visitors Scamper
One Eye Open, The Other Shut
I Hear The Scrunching Of A Chocolate Wrapper

As I Descend Into My Sleep,
Even There I Cannot Escape Them
I'll Shriek With A Morbid Fear
Of Choking In My Own Phlegm

The Thought Of These Vermin
Brown And Hairy Like Speedsters
Infesting Wherever They May Roam
And When Food's In Abundance Occurs

These Creatures Ramble In The Shadows
Agile And Fast, Blink, They're Gone
Resilient Through The Test Of Time
Before Us Humans Came To Dawn

Hidden From The Light
Darting Across The Floors
Manoeuvring Along
Finding Crevices Which To Lay Their Spores

No Crumbs Go Unnoticed
They're Never Left Behind
Only Their Poop, That Is Secreted
Diseased, After They Have Dined

They Will Gorge Themselves
On A Banquet, A Smorgasbord
There Is No Place Unattended
Where Food, To Them Is Stored

They Are My Nightmare Visitors
Even When I'm Awake
Sticky Traps All Laid Out, I'll Get Those Critters
If It's The Last Job I'll Make

Their Infested Presence
Since The Dawn Of Time
Evidence Of Their Grit
Forever They Will Continue To Climb

Their Presence Will Outlive Time Itself
They Set Foot On This Planet
Long Before We Were Here
Will Remain On This Earth To Inhabit

I Will Try Not To Scream,
Though I Know May Seem Irrational
A Shiver Will Run Down My Spine
But My Bravery I Will Try To Instil

I Hear Them Feeding Upon Morsels
Of Scraps And Other Food Decay
In The Darkness But What's That Matter
Still, They Swarm, Will They Even Go Away

I Sense Tonight There'll Be No Sleep, For
These Nightmare Visitors Keep Me At Bay
I Am Human, I Shall Not Bow Down
Be Rest Assured It Is Me, They Will Obey

Wherever They May Trail
I'll Be One Step Ahead
In The Attics, Or Beneath The Tiles
I Will Rid, Before Heading Off To Bed

YOUR SONG

Woke Up This Morning Feeling Well Inspired
Wanted To Write You A Song
The Lyrics And Tune, Just In My Head
Will Get It To Paper, Before Too Long

But It's Something So Simple
I Thought You Might Like To Hear
With Verses, A Harmony Written For You
Writing This Song, Wishing You Were Near

Your Song, About The Things, Left Unsaid
When I Walked Away, Feeling Sorry
I Had To Make It Up, Take Me Back
Felt There's Was A Problem, Felt That It Was Me

My Guitar At Hand, Plucking At The Strings
Tried To Pen Down The Words,
But My Inspiration Seemed To Just Fail,
Slipping With Every Resonant Chord

A Song, To You, I Must Compile
With Music That Will Fill The Air
May Not Be A Number One Hit
Yet It's Something To Show I Still Care

The Music Comes To Life As
The Beat Feels Soothing To The Heart,
It Pounded With The Excitement
Thinking Now, May Make The Charts

Foot Tapping, Body In A Swayed Motion
Backing Music, Like Sounds From A Symphony
The Words Come Together, Thinking Of You
How You Inspired, All That You've Given Me

Your Song, I've Dreamed Up For You
With Touching Words, I'll Hope You'll Listen
Something Special To Show My Affection
And To Tell You, It's You I Am Missin

I Want To Step Back In Time
To A Time, Before All This Started
I Would Then Think Twice
About, Why We Separated, Parted

HANDLE WITH CARE

It's Been Broken Many Times
Hurt By The Ones You've Loved
Its Pieces Can Be Mended
Perhaps By A Kiss Or A Hug

Upon It Written "Handle With Care"
Treat With Compassion And Respect
Its Love, Do Not Take For Granted
Will Last A Lifetime, Without Neglect

Your Heart, A Precious Gift
You Can Share With Another
So Handle With Care And Love
Taking Care Not To Smother

Give It Room To Breathe And Grow
Nurture With Love And Always Cherish
Tend To It When It Fail
That Perhaps One Day, Will Perish

Handle With Care, And Save From Grief
If Ever Your Heart's Lies In Peril
May It Never Be Ripped Or Torn
Or Ever Sold To The Devil

Handle With Care
Should It Break Be Crushed Into Pieces
A Fragile Heart Can Never Mend
Cept For When Love To It Increases

When Into Fragmented Parts, It Divides
Like Glass That's Been Shattered,
Handle With Care, This Heart Within
And Life It Will Give, When Not Bruised Or Battered

How Do You Mend This Broken Heart
From The Misery And Despair,
From The Lies You Spread
Behind My Back, Was More Than I Could Bear

My Heart, Now An Empty Shell
Once Filled With Hope, Now Only Resentment
Handle With Care
And Treat, As It Was Meant

On The Surface, Like Any Other
Deep Inside, There, The Heartaches Begins
The Bitterness, That For Years, You
Manipulated, Like Some Puppet On Strings

REFLECTIONS ON THE WINDOW

As I Look Out From My Window Screen
A Reflection, Is What It Throws At Me
Who Is This Person, At Me, Staring
Perhaps A Vision Of Who I Might Be

This Piece Of Glass, From My Window Pane
The Glare Into My Eyes Was Blinding
An Image Upon My Sight It Did Send
Then I Saw Stars That Were Shining

I Felt The Room Was Turning
Dazed Into A Sudden Dismay
I Couldn't Find My Bearing, Or Even Stand At All
Thinking, How Did I Get This Way

Reflections On The Window
Why Do You Stare My Way
All I See Are The Wrinkles, Upon My Face
I Wish They Would Go Away

No Hair, Where It Once Was
A Reminder, That I'm Now An Aging Soul
With Images Of Not How I Once Looked
I Feel You Have Taken Control

Reflections On The Window
Are You The Mirror Of My Life?
A Visual Echo, A Reminder
As Seen Through My Weary Eyes

Something Seems Different, Unsure What It Is
As It's Glancing Right My Way
I Know That It's Me, It's Looking At
I Try, But Can't Quite Turn Away

Like Magnetism It Pulls Me In
But The Reflection On The Window
Does Not Fade
It Only Hides Behind A Shadow

I See My World, From A Reflected Window Pane
As Upon It, The Light Does Shine
With The Colours Of The Spectrum
That I Could Never Define

As The Sun Goes Down,
The Reflections On The Window Will Disappear
Will Wait Another Day
For Them To Once Again Reappear

ACCEPT ME FOR WHAT I AM

I Don't Own A Fancy Car, A Mansion On A Hill
Jewellery To Be Adorned In
A Poor Family, My Sister, A Brother And I
Only Have Each Other, How It's Always Been

Accept Me For What I Am
I Shan't Be Anyone Else
Or That Someone You Want Me To Be
I Am Me, Nothing More, Nothing Less

I Have Failed, I Have Many Times Fallen
But I Got Up To Face My Fears
At Times Success Has Come My Way
Held With Both Hands, Still Sometimes Disappears

But I Keep On Trying, It's Who I Am
I Will Never Accept Defeat
When Hope Is By My Side
Who I Am, Has Made My Life Complete

Accept Me, For What I Am
For Who I Am, And Wanting To Achieve
See Me As Your Equal And Nothing Less
In Return, My Friendship You Will Receive

I Am Me, That's Who I Am
There's Never More I Want To Be
So Just Accept The Me That Is
Coz Deep Inside, It's My Heart You Will See

I Bleed Just Like You Do, When I'm Hurt
Laugh And Cry The Same
I Am The Product Of My Father, Mother
Hence The Person I Became

Please Accept Me For What I Am
A Reflection Of The Most Divine
Created To Share This World With You
In Its Goodness, That's How It Was Designed

When I Let Go Of Who I Am
I'll Become Someone That I Am Not
Accept Me For What I Am
It's The Only Me I've Got

Behind My Smile, There Are Those Tears
How To Be Accepted And Not Be Denied
Except Me As The Same
Together A Love We Will Find

DARKNESS IN THE WOODS

On A Foggy And Mystic Night
An Estranged Eerie Feeling Dawned Upon My Senses
With No Direction I Cried Out For You
Could You Not Hear Me, Beyond The Forest Edges

Cold Air Sent Shivers Down My Spine
The Darkness In Woods, Relentless
Critters Scurry To The Sounds Of Rustling Leaves
Here I Am, A Lonely Girl, Defenceless

Against The Chilling Night Breeze
To Hold You, And Wished You Were Near
To Comfort And Hold
Dying Here Alone Is One I Shall Fear

We Parted, You Told Me To Leave
An Argument, Words, So Foolishly Shared
I Begged For You To Take Me Back
Forgave You, Though The Things You Had Said

Darkness In The Woods, Like A
Canvas Backdrop With Stars Speckled,
Trees Arching Ten Stories High
And Forest Floors Settled

I Fought To Seek Refuge Under A Giant Oak
It Was Gonna Be A Cold Night
Broken And Torn, A Body On Blistered Feet
Must Keep Warm, With No Matches To Ignite

Over And Over, "I Must Keep Alive"
As The Midnight Hour Will Soon Fall Upon Me
Then Twilight Will Set The Skies Ablaze
But Not A Glimmer Of Hope, Do I See

The Darkness In The Woods
Dims My Sight, I Cannot See, Just Total Black
The Scent Of Fresh Bark, From The Trees Fallen
Has Before Me Stacked

I Go To Sleep And Dream Of Him
Will He Return, Or In His Arms Fall
My Eyelids Fall Heavy
Will He Take Me Back, And If I Must…Crawl

RUBBER BAND

Wrapped Around My Fingers
All Brown And Elastic Like
And as a Viper
When It's Ready To Strike

When Stretched Thin To
Its Breaking Point
A Sounding Snap As It Breaks
Will Surely Not Disappoint

With A Sharp Release
Slight And Thin
When Around My Fingers
The Fun, Just About To Begin

But Oh, What Amusement Can Be Had
This Bouncing Rubber Band
It May Seems Tiny
But Is Always Close At Hand

It Bounces When It Falls
Such A Playful Thing
Wrap It Around Your Fingers
Wait For It, Soon It Will Spring

For What Purposes Does It Serve
Rightfully So, You May Ask
Flick It, And It May Well
Zoom On Passed

Tie Your Hair, Or A Bracelet You'll Make
Holding Things Together
Or Maybe Repair A Paper Tear
Sturdy And Strong, Yet Light As A Feather

Whenever You May Need It
A Silly Poem About A Rubber Band
But You'll Agree It All Seems Fit
Wherever, Whenever It Will Land

This Rubber Band, Small, Yet Strong
Whatever The Occasion
Will Stretch To Its Limits
And Adapting To Any Situation

Watch It, And Will Bounce Back
A Slingshot Or Even A Catapult
Whatever You Fancy, This Humble Rubber Band
Keep It Close, And Never Be Set Apart

With A Snap, A Twang As tension mounted
Quick, Run And Hide
It Will Find You, I Promise
Escape, I Know You Would Have Tried

With A Echoing Ouch!
It Found Its Target
Its Mark, It Had Left Behind
But Hey! Will Only Hurt For Just Bit

DREAM AFTER DREAM

Dream after dream
Just fragmented images of our thoughts
What we hope will be, or one day become
Or at least be as we ought

Resting My Head Against The Pillow
I'm Cast Into A Deep Slumber, There I Cannot Hide
From The Nightmares, Dream After Dream
Where Fantasy And Reality, Collide

I Drift Further And Further In
And Trying To Take Control,
But My Body, Paralysed, Numb
As If Something, Was Engulfing Me Whole

This Timeless Journey To Who Knows Where
There Is No Escaping This Darkness
With Images Of Life Bombarding Me
How To Escape From This Madness

Just The Other Night, You Came
When I Was Asleep, You Appeared So Real
But I Know It Was Just A Dream
Wanted To Hold You, Kiss You, Feel

They Were Those Sleepless Nights
When I Wondered Where You Were
Dream After Dream, Kept Recurring
And Thinking, Losing You, Was More Than I Could Bear

When You Didn't Call Days Before
What Was I To Do, But Worry
I Dreamt You Took Off Your Ring
And Swore You Would Never Leave Me

I'd Dread If Dreams Ever Came True
And Knowing Nothing To Live For
My Life Would Be Nothing
If Life Could Not Offer More

Dream After Dream These Mere Illusions
Eating Up My Subconsciousness
Some To Remember, Some To Forget
Please Awaken Me, Please Promise Me This

When The 6am Clock Alarm Alerts
Awaiting For It To Chime
Waking In A Drenching Sweat
So, Into The Shower I must Climb

THE FARMER AND THE SEED

Every Morning, He Awakens Early
Onto The Field To, Scatter His Seeds
Times Are Hard, Making A Living
This Farmer, Many Mouths To Feed

His Wife Besides Him, Ploughing Ditches
Upon Which To Sow The Grains
They Know It's A Gamble, But Must Carry On
To Cover His Acreage Plains

Hoping They Will Take, For The Coming
Months, Before The Drought
A Field Of Corn, If The Plantation Is Right
He Fears, Perhaps Another Season Without

He Sows His Seed, Embedded, Deeply Soiled
Awaiting Spring, Then Hope, They Will Flourished
Laboriously They Plant, Over The Scorched Earth
Will The Rains Come, They Can Only Wish

Many Of The Seeds Swept To The Wind
In The Swirl Of The Breeze
Others Fell To The Ground Or Withered
In Desperation He Falls To His Knees

For The Farmer And Seeds, Time's Against Them
The Winds Pick Up, Dust Upon Their Eyes
But Must Carry On To Sow
Not Yet Noon, The Sun Slowly Rises

The Starlings, Overhead, Waiting For Their Feed
He Knows Soon, The Locust Plague
Causing Havoc To Plants And Fields
Thinks Of The Sacrifices, He Will Make

But He Knows If The Harvest Is Good
They Will Prosper, In The Months Coming
When They Will Take To The Fields To Plough
The Hard Work Would've Been For Something

Seasons Came, The Fields In Full Bloom
Coated In Silk, Coloured In Yellow And Green
Sprouting, Came Bearing Their Fruit
Now Time For The Harvesting Machine

SOMEONE DIFFERENT

Have You Ever Felt You Were Someone?
Different, Like You Didn't Belong
I Was That Kid, In A Playground Setting
Who Found It Hard To Get Along?

A Lonely Boy, Where No One Came Near
With Sleep In My Eyes, From The Tears I Cried
Second Hand Toys And Tattered Clothes
But I Wore, What I Had With Pride

Scraps Of Food, Whatever I Could Find
You See, We Didn't Have Much
But Mummy Did Her Best For Me
To Give It Her Motherly Touch

I Am That Someone Different
That Stands Out In A Crowd
Where People Stopped And Stared
I Didn't Care, I Was Proud

I Never Complied With All The Rules
I Was To Be Me, That's How I Would Stay
I Swore, That I Would Never Change
Even If It Meant, Id Be Turned Away

I Am That Someone Different
I Breathe The Air You Do
My Feelings, Are Much Like Yours
I See Things, With A Different Point Of View

I'm An Outcast Of Society,
So, I'm Forever Being Told
Will Never Mount To Anything
But I Refuse To Be Controlled

So, When You Breathe Out Your
Hatred Onto Me
Do You Expect Me To Follow?
And Hope, That I Would Agree

I Am That Someone Different
Though Not Popular, I Do Agree
But Under The Same Blue Sky
I Have Lived, This, I'll Always Be

I Wish We Can Always Be Friends
To Joke And Frolic And Run
Like Kids In The Playground
Even When The Day Is Nearly Done

I May Look At The World
Through Rosey Coloured Glasses
Because, I Am Someone Different
Who Sees Everything As It Passes

Bizarre, Unique, Different
Yep! Certainly, Sounds Like Me
An Individual Character
I Hope You Will Get To See

Someone Different,
Is That Such A Bad Thing
To Be An Individual
With The Character That I Bring

I Don't Follow What Is Normal
Or Dictated By What Is Common
I Do As My Body So Pleases
Though At Times, I May Have Fallen

I Have Only To Myself To Answer To
And No Judgement Upon You Cast
I Will Not Infringe Upon Your Any Views
Or My Opinions Shall I Pass

There's Been Times I've
Felt Alone, And Times I Wanted To Cry
And Times When I Did Not Care
Or Gave A Bother To Try

THROUGH THE WINDOW

Through The Window
Like Travelling Into Another Dimension
A Different Time Zone
That Someone Forgot To Mention

Trekking To Some Unknown Portal
Perhaps A Parallel Existence
Much Similar To Ours
Light Years Away, Into The Infinite Distance

Through The Window Into The Depth Of Time
Is There A Past, Present Or Future
Or Perhaps Something Not Conceived
On A Bigger Scale, Much Grandeur

Do We Even Dare To Travel Through It.
Disappointed By What We May Find
What Will We Encounter If To Survive?
From The World We Left Behind

Through The Window Of Time
The Years Swiftly Rewound
Seeing Myself In My Mother's Womb
Floating In An Amniotic Cloud

A Seedling, Life Has Not Yet Begun
But Creation Is On Its Way
Slowly Forming, Growing
Will Emerge Soon, One Day

Like A Cosmic Trooper
Drifting Off Into Space
It's Peaceful Out Here, Serene
Cannot Disturb This Silence In This Place

All Around Me, Flashback
In This Body, That Is Me
I'm Feeling Being Lifted
And From This Flesh, Being Set Free

Drifting Into A Timeless Plane.
Where Behind Me, The Open Window,
That I've Just Fallen Through
Left In Confusion, Like Drifting In Limbo

A Lifeless Void All Around
Where Time Cannot Escape
Sealed In A Vacuum, Like A Black Hole
That Cannot Take Shape

I'm Drifting, Drifting To
Who Knows Where
Am I Living Some Fairytale
This So Real, I'm Starting To Scare

Perhaps Something From Childhood
This Sounds Too Familiar
Maybe Just A Dream
Would Make An Interesting Thriller

Like The Man Who Fell Through A Window
And Awoken From A Sleepless Ordeal
Hitting His Head Upon It
Before Realizing, All This Wasn't Real

KOALA UP IN THE TREES

Thought To Mean "No Drink" Or "No Water"
The Koala Up In The Trees
Will Feed Throughout The Day
A Quarter Its Body Weight With Ease

A Marsupial That Lives High On A Tree Top
Eating Leaves Of The Eucalyptus
I Look Above, And Hope It Wouldn't Drop

A Native To Australia, This Vast Land Of Ours
Dwindling In Population, Its Habitat In Ruins
Conservation, We Must Try And Quick
And Educate The Careless, Some Humans

The Koala, In The Trees, Nursing Its Joey
No Bigger Than A Jelly Bean, If You'd Only Just Look
It Sucks Upon Milk Whilst It Clings To A Pouch
More You Can Learn From A Library Book

A Life Upon The Trees, Sleeps The Day Away
Amongst The Scented Leaves, Their Gums
Clinging With Claws Of Length
Highly Territorial, When Anything Comes

These Furry Creatures, Just Look, How Adorable
Rounded Bodies, Ears Fluffed, An Oval Nose
Mostly Grey In Colour And Fuzzy
60 Cm Or More, 14kg When It Fully Grows

Cute And Cuddly You Will Agree
Like Teddy Bears, Though Not Really A Bear
A Relative Of The Wombat, Another Aussie Critter
There In The Bushes, Let Us Protect And Be Aware

Snuggled Up, Curled Up In A Bundle
The Koala Up In The Tree, Where It Slumbers
Safe From Prying Eyes
While Trees In Ever Decreasing Numbers

Look About When Driving Across
Many Can Be Seen On A Koala Crossing
Give Way And Share The Road
And Don't Forget To Wave Upon Them Passing

Seen At Times Piggy Backing Riding
A Safe Retreat For Little Junior
For Around A Year
Or Even At Times, Much Sooner

While The Mother Searches For Food
The Young Will Follow, Hopping Each Eucalyptus
Sometimes Will Forage The Forest Floors
Surely, Don't Wanna Miss This

Native To This Land Down Under
Many Far And Wide Will Come To See
You Too Can Save This Animals So
Adopt A Koala From Up In The Trees

YOU'RE NEVER TOO FAR

Affairs Of The Heart Are Not Ruled By Distance
In Thoughts, You're Never Too Far
One Call Away, Then Together In Moments
That Time, Will Be Ours

Though The Miles Across The Vast Seas
Separates Us, You're Never Too Far
Over The Oceans And Plains
I've Come To Admire All That You Are

We Have Never Met,
And Time Is Of No Essence
Yet Honey, How I Long To Be
Standing Face To Face In Your Presence

To Feel Your Tender Warmth
The Fragrance Of A Woman's Scent
When The Breeze Upon Me Falls
We Shall Be Together As It Is Meant

When That Day Comes That I Should Hold You
I Pray That We Shall Never Part
No Quakes, Tornado And Hurricanes
Shall Sever My Grip To Tear Us Apart

Please Know That I'll Always Be There
When You Whisper My Name
I Will Come Running
To Rekindle That Burning Flame

You're Never Too Far
When All I Think About Is You
Every Waking Hour, Amidst Those Sleepless Nights
Cos It Is You, I Have Come To Pursue

You're Never Too Far
I'd Wipe Away Your Tears
When You Fall I Will Shield You
Protect You From All Your Fears

I Spoke To You The Other Day
About Everything And Nothing
Your Voice, Soothing To My Ears
A Sense Of Calmness I Felt Becoming

Sleepless Nights, The Moon Lit Bright
As The Sun Descended Over The Horizon
Ungodly Hours, I'm Still Awake
And Soon, Morning Will Have Risen

The Hours Tick On By,
And Thinking You're Somewhere Out There
But Never Too Far
Every Thought This Distance I Cannot Bear

HAND IN HAND

We Are Black, White And Colours In Between
In A World Of Diversities, Mixed Races
Living Lives As One Should
From All Walks, Different Areas, Various Places

This Sphere That's Been Created
A Melting Pot Of Variety, The Poor, The Oppressed
With Them, Learn To Walk Hand In Hand
Our Brothers, Our Sisters And The Not So Blessed

We Grow Up Learning To Hate, What Reason?
Fight, Because Of Their Indifference
We All Bleed The Same Colour
So, Why Then, Ignore Their Existence

When A Child Will Ask "Mummy Why Is She Black"
"Just A Colour Honey" Must Love Her The Same"
Not Yet Able To Realise, But Can Be Nurtured
And To Feel No Shame

We're All The Same When Our Tears Fall
We All Smile When We Share The Laughter
Ain't No Reason We Gotta Fight
And Pay The Consequences After

Black Hand, White Hand Joint As One
All People, No Matter The Colour
When We Walk With Hate In Our Hearts
Love Is Lost With One Another

Look In The Mirror What Will One See
A Reflection Staring Back At You
Doesn't Care About The Skin Or Colour,
Your Life, Or What You've Gone Through

Cannot Erase The Past, For The Scars We Must Bear
Can Only Move Forward, Walking Hand In Hand
To Eradicate The Prejudice, The Judgement
And As One, This Hatred We Can Withstand

Prejudice, Like Cancer, Upon Us Grows
No Reasons, No Concepts, Just Hate The Different
The Black, The White, The Short, The Tall
No Respect To The Suffering

We Break Down The Hatred Barriers
When We First Walk Hand In Hand
With Neighbours, The Complete Strangers
We Then Learn To Understand.

TIME FREEZE

There's been a time, when time did not exist
A time, when nothingness was all that's been
The world we know, did come to be
Somewhere down the line, time did begin

Imagine, In this World, Where Time Stood Still
Where The Wind Stops Blowing
The Sun, Upon Us, Shone No More
Or The Water, From The Rivers, Stopped Running

People Around You, Frozen In A Solid State
No Heat To Keep Them Warm
And What If The Earth Stopped Turning
There'll Be No Air Of Any Form

Struggling For What Little Air To Breathe
Suffocating, Until Your Body Disintegrates
No Water To Clench Your Thirst
Death, Upon You Soon Awaits

If Time Did Freeze
The World Be Set Into An Infinite Darkness
As The Sun, Has Long Been Out
And If We Survived This, What Harm Will Come To Us

People Floating In The Air
As No Gravity To Keep Us Down
The Moon Has Drifted Out Into Space
And Will Not Be Turning Round

If Time Froze Over
No Sounds Can Be Heard
Assuming, You're Still Alive To Hear
But Just The Thought Of It, Seems Quite Absurd

The Hands Of The Clock, Stopped, What Then
Not A Second, Minute Or Hour, Goes By
They Just Stood Still
I Guess Then, Time Wouldn't Fly

If The Wheels Of Time Stopped Turning
No Future To Speak, Nothing To Expect
The Presence Stays The Same
You'd Not Grow Old, No Aging Defects

Time Freeze, You'd Better Hope Not
It Is Something, That Can Be Preserved
Take A Photo, And See The Past
Keep For Keepsake, To Later Observe

If The Hourglass Of Time Did Freeze
Who'd Be Left To Write This
No One To Write Their Thought And
This, I Would Surely Miss

WHAT MAY LIE AHEAD

Each New Day That Falls Upon This Earth
When The Dark Of Night, Makes Way, Shine Of The Day
And Stars Above Will Disappear
There Darkness Will Drift Away

I Don't Know The Hereafter
I Only Know The Past
I Don't Know What May Lie Ahead
Only That What's Gone, Is Now Passed

I Daren't Know, What Tomorrow Holds
A Cloudy Day, Dressed With Thunder Storms
What May Lie Ahead, Not So Sure
Perhaps A Sunny Day, Will Be Transformed

Let Fate Decide What Is Inevitable
That, Which Cannot Be Deflected
We May Skip Or Avoid The Hurdles
But In The End, Nothing Can Be Expected

We've Always Wished To Delve Into The Future
Perhaps To Win The Lottery
We Set Sights Beyond Our Expectations
And Cannot Accept, What Should Be

A Crystal Ball, We Will Upon It Gaze
Or Look To The Stars, The Moon And Sun
Or Tarot Cards We Will Read
But Is Knowing What's To Happen, At All Fun

Since The Beginning Of Time,
When It All Began
We Have Thrived To Figure What Lies Ahead
Going Back, Since The Dawn Of Man

We Cannot Know The Paths Of Our Lives
Or What May Lie Ahead
We'll Never Give Up Trying
To Get Out, What's In Our Head

We Take Our Chances, Mistakes Along The Way
We Will Fail Before We Succeed
Knowing What May Lie Ahead
Is Perhaps All That We Need

We Strive For Better Days
In The Events Forthcoming
What May Lie Ahead We Can Only Imagine?
And For Prosperity We'll Always Be Hoping

But With The Good Comes The Bad
Opportunities Will Come, Will Go
And What May Lie Ahead
We Shall Yet To Find Out, To Know

What May Lie Ahead
Is It Glory, Or Is It Gloom
I Wish I Knew The Answers
I Can Never Truly Know, But Only Assume

Am I Gonna Get Married
With A Happy And Contented Wife
Or Have Children At My Side
And Lead A Happy And Healthy Life

What May Lie Ahead
This, I Can Only Contemplate
I Cannot Know For Certain
But Hope I Knew, Before It Got Too Late

What May Lie Ahead, Only God Knows
This Journey We Must Undertake
The Journey Of Life
Where Sacrifice We Must Make

What May Lie Ahead,
Whatever May Be In Store
There, Chances We Will Take
For Opportunities To Open A New Door

If Only We Knew
What Before Us, May Lie Ahead
What's On The Other Side
Or Perhaps The Other End

Whatever It Is, That Lies Ahead
Will Be Beyond Our Spatial Reach
For Knowing What It Is
May Undoubtedly Make Our Lives Complete

SOMEWHERE ONLY WE KNOW

A World Apart, How Was She To Notice Me
Our Eyes Made Contact
As I Recall Back Then
And Remembering, How We'd Act

Childish Frolics, Holding Hands
Prancing Through Fields, To Her A Daisy
A Peck On Her Cheeks
Some May Have Called Us Crazy

We Didn't Care, We Had Each Other
That Day, Our Affection Spiralled
Promised This Would Last Forever
And Told Her, That It Was Her, I Desired

We Ventured Beyond The Woods
As The Many Times We Previous Had
To A Place Somewhere Only We Knew
A Magical Scene Holding Her Hand

Somewhere Only We Know
Where Giant Oaks Umbrella The Sky
Sheltering The Forest Floors
And The Scent Of Fresh Bark Peeling Away Dry

This Place, Where Wishes Come True
Here, Somewhere Only We Know
Like In Fairy Story Neverland
Where Peter Pan Would Go

This Was Our Fantasy Land
Only Read About In Children's Books
Where Fairies, Winged And Magical
Sprinkle Fairy Dust, When To Us They'd Look

Their Wings, Iridescent Crystal Blue
Like A Hummingbird On Take-off, Soundless
Grace To Flight To The Lily Pads
Just Above The Water's Surface

In The River Streams,
Where The Fluorescent Rainbows Swam
Fireflies Buzzing, They Are An Easy Prey
Looking Around And Wondering Where I Am

I Stopped To Admire, Not So Far Away,
Mermaids With Tails Shimmering
Vibrant Scales Of Blue Yellow And Greens
Blonde Hair Wavy, My Lusty Urges Quivering

Staring At Each Other
And Wondering What's Next
Leprechauns, Going About Their Day
Collecting Mushrooms, Looking Confused, Perplexed

We Waved To Say Hello
But Only Giggles From Them We Hear
As They Scurry Doing Daily Chores
In A Blink, They Slowly Disappear

Somewhere Only We Know
This Scenery Is Our Adventure Land
Where We Are Beautified By A Blessing Of Unicorns
Roaming The Fields So Majestic And Grand

Just Over The Hill
An Old Shack, Where Nobody Dares To Dwell
A Mottled Rustic Look About It
Drastic Need Of Repair To Rid Its Pungent Smell

And Somewhere Only We Know
That Will Not Extinguish Our Hopes Our Dreams
We Do Not Age But Feel Forever Young
And Just Like, Living In Our Teens

Growing Old Is A Thing Of The Past
Where The Hands Of Time Unwound
No Wrinkles Upon Your Face
And Here, Freedom's Unbound

Somewhere Only We Know
A Familiar Place Beyond The Here And Now
Beyond Tomorrow, In A Land Of Fantasy
Can Be Yours, Only If Your Imagination Will Allow

THAT FIRST KISS

Boy Meets Girl, And So The Story Goes
A Twinkle In Their Eyes,
But Wasn't Always That Way
But Over Time, They Began To Realize

There Was Something Special, Something Unique
At Their Age, Who Would Have Known
That Maybe Someday, Turns To Be More
This Love, Would Be Their Own

In Closeness, Body To Body
Shortened Breath, Palms Sweated
"May I Kiss You?" Thought You'd Never Ask
Moistened Lips, Wetted

Gently, Softly Touching
That First Kiss, They Lock Lips
Like A Symphony, Slowly Building
Excites Her Quivering Hips

She Was, His Childhood Sweetheart
No-One Thought This To Last
But She, All He's Ever Known
And To Make Her His, This He Must

That First Kiss, Like A Bee To Honey
Sweetest Nectar From You I Sip
Flowing Juices, With Emotions Flow
Let Us Go On A Journey, On A Lovers Trip

That Moment, Her Eyes Twinkled
Would Light Any Dark Nights
Wanted So Much To Hold Her, Still
Until The Fire Within Me Ignites

Like Butterflies, Our Stomachs Fluttered
While Tongues Flicked, Became Entwined
Didn't Want This To Stop
Our Bodies, For This, So Designed

Only Left Me Wanting More
And This Day, This Moment, To Never End
We Were Gasping For Air
While Thinking, More Time With Her I'd Spend

Like A Deluge, I Was Swept Away By Her
Like Rivers Racing To The Sea
A Beauty, Unsurpassed
I Knew, Her And I Were Meant To Be

Her Softened Skin, Pressing Against Mine
Hearts Beating, The Blood Would Rush
We Were Cheek To Cheek
When, Against Her Chest, My Hands Would Touch

That Moment In Time, Seemed A Life Time
And This Was Our First Kiss
Now Wondering, What Is Yet In Stored
That May Send Us Into A Heavenly Bliss

SOMETIMES

Sometimes We Don't Understand

The Reasons, Things

Happen, But

Do

We Quickly Realise The

Choices We Make Can Be Life

Changing

A Different Perspective,

Sometimes A Different Point Of

View

There Are Times, We'll Make

Wrong Choices, Leads To Life

Re-Arranging

Sometimes Our Actions Define

Who We Are Or

Become

But On The Path Of Life, The Choices

We Make Are The Chances We

Take

And To Our Destiny The

Future Is What's Yet To

Come

Ahead Of Us, Opportunities,

To Learn From Our

Mistakes

Sometimes In Our Failures

We Make Vague

Excuses

Apologise For An Action

Wrongly

Taken

In Times Of Our Lives, It's

Hard Accepting, Knowing, What The

Truth Is

Along The Way, We Are Guided

By Free Will And Decision

Making

regret

BROKEN DREAMS

I Was Young And Naïve
When My Dreams Were Many
But None, Have I Achieved
Do Any Exist, If Any?

Those Sleepless Nights, I Lay Awake
Wondering, Where My Life Will Lead
So Much I Want To Achieve
How Or When, Will I Succeed

This Journey, Many Times I've Travelled
Along This Same Road Of Desperation
What Lay Ahead, Had The Same Old Story
But Needing To Assess My Situation

Broken Dreams, Came Recurring
Like A Film On Rewind
Again And Again, Unstopping
But Nothing In Here, Will I Find

I Remained Here, Picking Up Fragments
Of Broken Dreams, That Failed To Come True
Every Ambition, Deserted Me
Left Me Stranded, Torn In Two

And Like A Broken Heart That's Shattered
Much Like These Broken Dreams
Never Will To Mend, Though Piece By Piece
Cannot Restore My Self Esteem

I Will Not Yield To Barricades
Nor Fall To The Ground In Defeat
They Shall Not Weary Me By Chains
And Never Will, My Fury Release

Like A China Doll That's Been Broken,
And Delicately Rebuilt
Broken Dreams Can Be Restored
Only If My Aspirations Were To Exist

With Broken Dreams, crumbled
Into A Thousand Portions
Like A Jigsaw Puzzle, with Missing Pieces
Every Angle I Seek, That Laid In Distortion

Somewhere In My Mind
In A World Of Broken Dreams
This Lonely Boy, Walks Alone
Trying To Figure Out, What All Of This Means

With Nobody To Turn To
All My Hopes And Desires Gone
Forlorn, Fierce Anger Taunting
And From Society, I Became Withdrawn

I Looked For Signs, But Nothing Found
Into The Sky, A Ray Of Light
Could This Mean Something
Which, Might Make Things Right

Upon My Expectation I Could Not Rely
Buried, Somewhere Within, Confined
I Needed Relief, To Set Me Free
From A Bewildered Mind

Broken Dreams, Leaving Me In A Fury State
Raged With Patches Scattered
I Know There Is No Escape
When My Thoughts Become Wasted

I Cannot Help This Feeling Of Rejection,
Beaten By These Broken Dreams
I Know They Can Be Rebuilt
And Some Day, I Will Reign Supreme

BURNING WORDS

Like A Blazing Fire That Slowly Burns
Destruction, Soon To Unfold
Cannot Be Stopped, Once To The Wind It Takes
Just Like Words, At Times, Uncontrolled

There Are Times
Words, I've Been Meaning To Say
But Got All Choked Up
In How I Must Convey

In Anger, Burning Words Did Ignite
They Leapt From My Lips
Like Flames Sputtering In Gasoline
No Intention Of Harm, To Her, Did I Inflict

Words Can Find Solace
When In Grief And In Despair
Can Cut Like A Knife To Butter
Build Walls To Show That You Care

Burning Words That Scald The Heart
With Its smouldering Fiery Heat
Will Burn Intently Deep Inside
Till Your Body Has Found Defeat

I Spoke Some Words
How I Wished I Could Retract
When In Haste So Quickly Acted
But Once Said, There's No Going Back

Its Burden, That I Must Now Bare
Of Knowing You Mayn't Return
I Dearly Tried To Apologise
But I Guess You Never Heard

Though I, Of Foolish Mind,
Can Admit My Wrong Doing
And The Hurts, Too Much To Bear
Yet Still, It Is Your Love I Am Pursuing

I Know There Is Hope
In The Silence That Lies Between Us
Can We Embrace, As In The Yesteryears Did
And Tomorrow Be As Yesterday Was Once

Let Me Build What Has Been Torn
Or Ignite That Candle Blown Out,
And Rekindled What I Must Enflame
It Is You, After All, I Cannot Do Without

In The Storms Of Words Loosely Spoken
The Warmth We Shared Are A Distant Dream
Those Words, Now Lost In Time
But Still, Tears From My Eyes Do Stream

I Cannot Control What I Feel
Hurting You Was Never Intended
Those Burning Words, Like A Whisper Carries
Into The Wind That Never Ended

Burning Words So Deep And Harsh
A Cruel Reminder Of What We Can Lose
One Moment We Can Cherish
Then We Fall To Abuse

And Even Though Words
Can Burn The Heart
Too, Scorch Like A Burning Flame
they can also soothe or drift us apart

HIS FINAL POEM

He Sits Uninspired, At His Desk
Waste Paper Basket Filled To The Brim
Failed Attempts To Write His Final Poem
The Future For This Poet Looks Grim

With Scribbled Notes Barely Legible Upon His Pad
Filled Up Quill, Ink Blots Splattered
And Words That Connect
Only Leaves His Ambitions Battered

His Final Poem, What Is It To Be
His Life, Perhaps, As A Failed Poet
A Failed Writer That No One Got To Read
And If They Did, They Never Really Showed It

Lines Upon His Face,
That Shows A Life Of Anguish
What Might Be His Final Poem? Like A Flame
Put Out, So Too, His Thoughts Extinguished

Smoke Fills The Room, Butts Overflowing
Yellow Stains Upon His Fingers
An Old JD, By His Side,
The Putrid Scent Of The Air Lingers

The Clock Chimes 2 In The Morning
When Suddenly A Sentence, A Line
A Glimmer Of Hope, An Inspiration
But Still Nothing Comes To Mind

The Window Blows Open
A Gust Swirls, Sending Papers Flying
Frantically Collecting What Little Evidence
To Continue On Trying

He's An Aging Poet, Sight Growing Dim
Must Do All That He Can
If He At Least Gets To See Another Day
So Decides To Finish What He Began

Into The Morning Hours, Clock Ticking By
The Rooster Crows The 5am Call
Dogs On The Streets Barking
Progress, He's Made, Though Seems Small

A Page, Now Filled With Words
As He Begins To Read, He Smiles
This He Wonders, Is A Life
Of A Poet, With Its Tribulations And Trials

With His Quill In His Hand, he's found Dead
The Following Morning
Head Upon His Final Poem
With The Title, "My Last" Was Forming

A Service Was Held, That Few Would Attend
A Eulogy, Words Of Condolences About Him
That No One Barely Heard
How He Struggled To Write His Final Poem

THE PAINTING

There It Sits Upon An Easel Stand
Devoid Of Colour, Whitened, Blank
A Canvas Board Awaiting Its Master's Hands
And Soon Later, His Artistry, We'll Thank

Like A Conductor's Baton
His Brush, With Vivid Stroke Forms
The Painting Begins To Emerge
And Into A Scene, It Will Transform

Swirling Colours In A Whirling Blaze
Crimson Reds Shadowed The Midnight Blue
A Sunset Scene, Beyond The Horizon
In The Distance, Night Birds Flew

Sparkling Stars In The Night Sky Shone
Rippled Oceans, Clashing Upon Metamorphic Rocks
The Artist, Standing Back, Begins To Admire
And From His Imagination Visions Unlock

The Painting, At The Mercy Of The Palette
With The Colours, In An Impressive Array
Orange And Blues, The Violets And All Other Hues
In Awe, Smiles At The Perfection Is Displayed

Like Magic Before His Eyes
Shaping From Nothing To This Masterpiece
A Work In Progress, With Pigmented Strokes
Perhaps Another Henri Matisse

His Dreams Are Many, But To Sell Just One
His Name In Limelight, As The Before Greats
The Painting, He Will Make Immortal
To Live Through The Ages, Only Time Awaits

Paint Smeared, Drizzled, Eyes Blinded
But Must Carry On To Finish, Complete
Eyes smouldering In A Rage Of Anger
He Soldiers On, And Will Accept No Defeat

The Painting, Upon That Easel Rests
In A Studio, Surrounded By Many Others
Oils And Acrylic, Pastels And Chalk
In A Rainbow Spectrum Of Various Colours

In A Surge Of Ambition, Enthusiasm Flying
Like An Artist, A Writer, A Well-Rehearsed Poet
Filled With Visions, Perhaps Illusions
But The Painter Knows To What He Must Commit

Pallet Knife In Hand, Oils He Mixes
Finishing Touches, Are In His Sight
The Painting Now Hangs In The Louvre
As this verse, that I write

THIS SMALL TOWN

A Boy, A Girl In Their Own Little Part Of Town
Separate Lives, And To Nobody They Belonged
A Derelict Town Where No One Ever Goes
And Nobody, Daren't Travel Beyond

One Yester Summer, Hot And Scorched
Upon The Beach, They Happened To Stumble
And As Fate Had It, They Would Chat
But Only To Find, Their Words Would Crumble

Packed With Nerves Shattered
Sweat Flowing From Their Brows
Tongues Tied, That
No Words, Would Their Voices Allow

This Was No Romeo And Juliet
But A Love Story In The Making
She Was Eighteen, And He Twenty
But For Each Other, Their Hearts Were Aching

This Small Town, Where Sidewalks
Were Paved With Cracks And Grooves
Looking Like Some Bomb Had Hit
But Hope, From Here, One Day They Would Move

Now, Barely Anyone Lives Here
Who Would Want To, After All
Or Care To Admit, Least For This Couple
Who For Each Other, They Would Fall

They Had No Dreams To Live For
Working At Dead End Positions
Jobs Paid Little In Wages
And Tolerating Such Conditions

This Small Town
Very Few, Came To Live Or Visit
No One Knowing, This Place Existed
Perhaps Not On Any Map, Or Is It

They Made Plans To Move
Away From This Small Town
To The City, Where Life, Never Closes
Where It Was Easier To Get Around

From This Small Town
Where Rumours Would Spread
Like Chinese Whispers, A Fire In A Breeze
Uncontrollable, As The Words That Were Said

This Small Town, Where Everyone
Knows Your Name
What You Do, Or What You Say
Nothing's Sacred, No One Is Free From Blame

From This Small Town
They Packed Their Things And Left
Leaving Behind memories
And What Little They Possessed

But For This Little Town
It Will Be Forgotten, Seldom Missed
Phasing Out Through The Ages,
As If It Never Did Exist

FOOTPRINTS IN THE SAND

The Musky Sea Breeze
The Scent Of The Salted Air
Upon Our Faces Slowly Caressing The Pores
And Sand Grit Blew Upon Our Hair

As We Walked Upon The Gritty Beach
In That Summer Of Yesteryear
Blessed With Our Youth, Always Dared To Dream
And Weren't Controlled By Fear

Unafraid To Take Our Chances
Forgetting About What Might Happen
Did We Even Care, When All We Knew,
That Love Was So Blind, Back Then

Our Feet Slowly Sank, Leaving Footprints In The Sand
Then Drifted Away, With The Rolling Tide
Yet Still We Frolicked, Like Children Might
Those Moments In Time, Would Not Be Denied

Riding Upon The Crest Of The Waves
Seaweed Gathered At Our Feet
As Sand between Our Toes gathered
When The Sun Bared Down Its Afternoon Heat

Those Footprints In The Sand
Now Long Forgotten In The Pages Of Time
That Came, That Went,
But Still, Every Moment We Climbed

If The Second Hands Of Time Stood Still
I'm Sure That Those Moments Also Did,
As We Gazed In Each Other's Eyes
Our Emotions, We Would Not Forbid

Promises We Shared, And Vowed Never To Break
I Am To You, That Trusted Friend
To Follow You, If Ever Be Lost
Unlike Those Footprints In The Sand

When You Need A Shoulder To Cry Upon
I'll Promise To Be There
Or Weary, With A Heavy Laden Heart, I'll Be There
I'll Be There, To Mend, If Ever In Despair

Those Footprints In The Sand
Like Sandcastles Upon That Beach, Diminished
Crumbled Away Never To Stay,
With Every Rippled Tide, That Hit

As I Watched Them Fade Away
Wishing Those Footprints Lay Unfazed
By The Tides, That Rippled Onto Shore,
Upon That Beach My Eyes, To Them I Gazed

Those Days, Sadly Now The Past
While Only My Memories Of Them Uphold
And Those Footprints In The Sand
Remains My Story To Be Told

WHAT ONCE WAS

We Took For Granted Instances We Shared
But Knew, May Never Again Be Upon Us
We Relished In That Past
Now Will Take Time To Adjust

What Once Was,
We Lived In Those Few Moments
Just Like Time, It Came And It Went
Will Always Treasure, Those Very Instants

The Here And Now, What More Have We
What Once Was Made Possible
Is Only Time Left Squandered
And Time Is Never A Guarantee

What Once Was
Is As Precious As The Air We Inhale
Use Wisely, Before All Will Be Gone
Treasured Memories, Will Not Always Prevail

In The Times Of What Once Was
They Were Not Mine, But Ours
When We Frolicked Like Kids Might
And Showered You, With Petaled Flowers

Childish Pranks We Played
We Etched Our Names Upon A Tree
That Tree Has Now Grown
But Our Memories Will One Day Be Free

"Remember This Moment" I Uttered From My Lips
I Knew, They'd Seldom Last Forever
Every Instance, I Grasped And Held
Not Wanting To Let Go, Never

What Once Was, Could Never Bring Back
As Time Phases Crept On By
A Second, A Minute Or An Hour
Watch, As Before Us, Would Fly

The Happiness, I Once Had
How Can I Bring It Back Now
And Rid From Upon Me, This Pain
If Only I Could, Just Not Knowing How

Turning Back Time, If Only That Be True
I'd See Your Face, Your Smile
I Needn't Worry, Of What Once Was
Cos In My Heart, I'd Be With You Awhile

To Live Our Lives Throughout,
To Cherish And Embrace
And Light The Fire Of Life, When Together
Take On, Whatever The Future Awaits

Or What Once Was, Time's Fragmented Reflection
When Two Lovers, Their Hearts Pounding
Who Treasured The Short Moment's Every Second
And All Around Them, Their Joys Resounding

What Once Was, Already, We Know
What Will The Future Have In Store
Perhaps Something Not Yet Learnt
But Who Can Really Tell Anymore?

What Once Was,
Perhaps Will Always Remain
That Outcome, Seldom Ever Changes
Or One, We'll Never See Again

WHAT REALLY MATTERS

We Think About Things, We Know Very
Little About
But Do We Think Of Things That Really Matter
To Which There Is Not Doubt

Is There A God Or A Heaven Above
When We Leave And Perish This Earth
Or A Devil In His Infernal Hell
Does What Really Matters Have Its Worth

I've Often Wondered
Where Do We Go, When Our Lives Have Ended
And Of The Judgement Day As In The Bible
And When Jesus, To Heaven Ascended

The Man That Walked The Earth
Who Died To Forgive Our Sins
So That We May Live
And Into Heaven Where A New Life Begins

What Really Matters On The Scheme Of Things
The Clothes We Wear, Or The Car We Drive
The Money We Must Earn To Be Successful
So That Our Lives May Thrive

What Really Matters, When That Day Comes
To Meet Our Creator
Will We Come Back As A Cat, A Dog Reincarnated
Or Perhaps Someone Else, We'll Find Out Later

Many Questions, That Cannot Be Answered
In This Scope Of This Universe, Our Milky Way
In It Immense Vastness, The Never Ending
Its Distance, So Far Away

We'll Probe At Question After Questions
As To Why And How, We Came To Be
In A World Of Billions, That Roam This Earth
I Cannot, This Answer Tell You, Not That I Can See

We Worry About The Things We Cannot Control
The Weather, Or Whether We Live Or Die
Death Is Inevitable, This I Guarantee
Just Live Life, And Don't Ask Why

Do We Really Care About Our Brothers?
Sister Or Our Neighbours Near
Are They What Really Matters:
And Truly, Do We Hold Them Dear

What Is It, That Mostly Matters
It Isn't The Thunder On A Stormy Night
But The Silence That Soon Will Follow
And Then, From The Heavens, Soon To Be Light

Is What Really Matters In Life
That We Have To Pay For Our Dues
Each Day We Take For Granted
Like How We Treat Others, If We So Choose

This Question May Seem An Enigma
When At Times We Have No Guidance
What Really Matters Now
Is That With Nature And Life, There Will Be Compliance

BOWING TO THE QUIET LIGHT

I've Learnt To Bow On Bended Knees
The Strength Within Had Found Grace
A Quality In Man, One Often Not Sees

Bowing To The Quiet Light
My Voice Softly Spoken
I've Learnt To Bow On Bended Knees

They Don't Yet Hear Me
As My Eyes Softly Look Up
A Quality In Man, One Often Not See

I'm Always There To Solely Please
In A Good Will Gesture, I Will Embrace
I've Learnt To Bow On Bended Knees

Respect, As It Seems, Many Will Agree
None As This, Will I Ever Replace
A Quality In Man, One Often Not Sees

So Let My Reverence Be The Key That Frees
Humility That I Own, One Cannot Replace
I've Learnt To Bow On Bended Knees
A Quality In Man, One Often Not Sees

www.ingramcontent.com/pod-product-compliance
Lightning Source LLC
Chambersburg PA
CBHW052005070526
44584CB00016B/1626